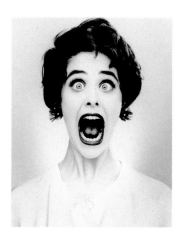

Pro·Lighting

PORTRAITS

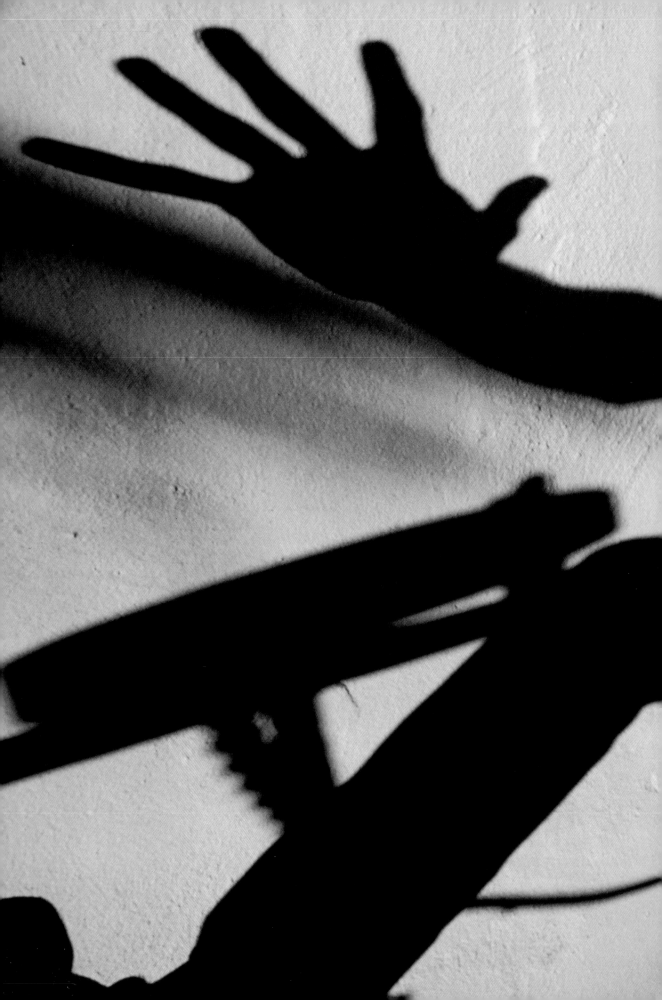

Pro·Lighting

ROGER HICKS and FRANCES SCHULTZ

PORTRAITS

ROTOVISION

A Quarto Book

Published and distributed by:
RotoVision SA
7 rue du Bugnon
1299 Crans
Switzerland

RotoVision SA Sales Office
Sheridan House
112/116A Western Road
Hove, West Sussex BN3 IDD
England
Tel: +44 1273 72 72 68
Fax: +44 1273 72 72 69

Distributed to the trade in the United States:
Watson-Guptill Publications
1515 Broadway
New York, NY 10036

ISBN 2-88046-273-8

This book was designed and produced by
Quarto Publishing plc
6 Blundell Street
London N7 9BH

Creative Director: Richard Dewing
Designer: Fiona Roberts
Senior Editor: Anna Briffa
Editor: Kit Coppard
Picture Researchers: Roger Hicks and Frances Schultz

Typeset in Great Britain by
Central Southern Typesetters, Eastbourne
Manufactured in Singapore by Teck Wah Paper Products Ltd.
Printed in Singapore by ProVision Pte. Ltd.
Tel: +65 334 7720
Fax: +65 334 7721

CONTENTS

▼

▼

THE MOST COMMON RESPONSE FROM THE PHOTOGRAPHERS WHO CONTRIBUTED TO THIS BOOK, WHEN THE CONCEPT WAS EXPLAINED TO THEM, WAS "I'D BUY THAT." THE AIM IS SIMPLE: TO CREATE A LIBRARY OF BOOKS, ILLUSTRATED WITH FIRST-CLASS PHOTOGRAPHY FROM ALL AROUND THE WORLD, WHICH SHOW EXACTLY HOW EACH INDIVIDUAL PHOTOGRAPH IN EACH BOOK WAS LIT.

Who will find it useful? Professional photographers, obviously, who are either working in a given field or want to move into a new field. Students, too, who will find that it gives them access to a very much greater range of ideas and inspiration than even the best college can hope to present. Art directors and others in the visual arts will find it a useful reference book, both for ideas and as a means of explaining to photographers exactly what they want done. It will also help them to understand what the photographers are saying to them. And, of course, "pro/am" photographers who are on the cusp between amateur photography and earning money with their cameras will find it invaluable: it not only shows the standards that are required, but also the means of achieving them.

The lighting set-ups in each book vary widely, and embrace many different types of light source: electronic flash, tungsten, HMIs, and light brushes, sometimes mixed with daylight and flames and all kinds of other things. Some are very complex; others are very simple. This variety is very important, both as a source of ideas and inspiration and because each book as a whole has no axe to grind: there is no editorial bias towards one kind of lighting or another, because the pictures were chosen on the basis of impact and (occasionally) on the basis of technical difficulty. Certain subjects are, after all, notoriously difficult to light and can present a challenge even to experienced photographers. Only after the picture selection had been made was there any attempt to understand the lighting set-up.

This book is a part of the third series: PORTRAITS, STILL LIFE and NUDES. The first series was PRODUCT SHOTS, GLAMOUR SHOTS and FOOD SHOTS, and the second was INTERIORS, LINGERIE and SPECIAL EFFECTS. The intriguing thing in all of them is to see the degree of underlying similarity, and the degree of diversity, which can be found in single discipline or genre.

In portraiture, for example, there is a remarkable preference for monochrome and for medium formats, though the styles of lighting are very varied. In nudes, softer lighting is more usual, though the rendition is very often what painters would call 'hard edge'. And in still lifes, although few manipulated images are shown in the book, many photographers said that they were already doing this or were getting in to it.

In none of the books of the third series, though, is there as much of a 'universal lighting set up' as was so often detectable in the first two series. This is probably because all three topics are inclined to be personal pictures, often portfolio shots, and therefore reflect artistic variety more than commercial necessity.

The structure of the books is straightforward. After this initial introduction, which changes little among all the books in the series, there is a brief guide and glossary of lighting terms. Then, there is specific introduction to the individual area or areas of photography which are covered by the book. Subdivisions of each discipline are arranged in chapters, inevitably with a degree of overlap, and each chapter has its own introduction. Finally, at the end of the book, there is a directory of those photographers who have contributed work.

If you would like your work to be considered for inclusion in future books, please write to Quarto Publishing plc, 6 Blundell Street, London N7 9BH, England, and request an Information Pack. DO NOT SEND PICTURES, either with the initial inquiry or with any subsequent correspondence, unless requested; unsolicited pictures may not always be returned. When a book is planned which corresponds with your particular area of expertise, we will contact you. Until then, we hope that you enjoy this book, that you find it useful, and that it helps you in your work.

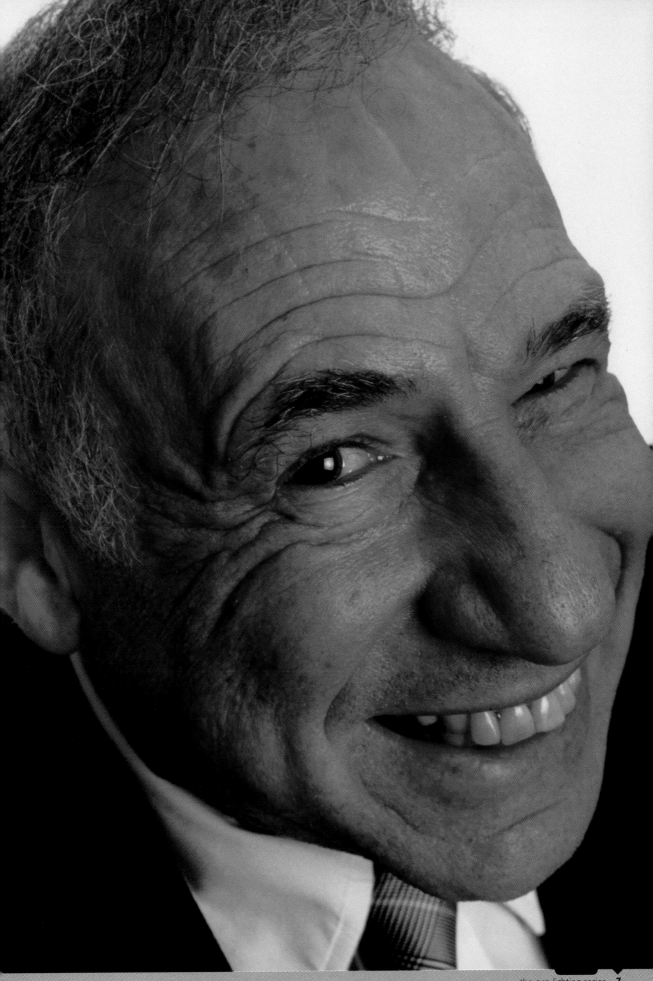

HOW TO USE THIS BOOK

▼

THE LIGHTING DRAWINGS IN THIS BOOK ARE INTENDED AS A GUIDE TO THE LIGHTING SET-UP RATHER THAN AS ABSOLUTELY ACCURATE DIAGRAMS. PART OF THIS IS DUE TO THE VARIATION IN THE PHOTOGRAPHERS' OWN DRAWINGS, SOME OF WHICH WERE MORE COMPLETE (AND MORE COMPREHENSIBLE) THAN OTHERS, BUT PART OF IT IS ALSO DUE TO THE NEED TO REPRESENT COMPLEX SET-UPS IN A WAY WHICH WOULD NOT BE NEEDLESSLY CONFUSING.

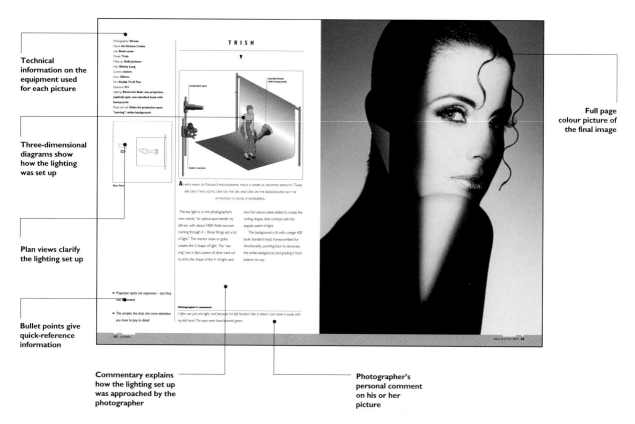

Technical information on the equipment used for each picture

Three-dimensional diagrams show how the lighting was set up

Plan views clarify the lighting set up

Bullet points give quick-reference information

Full page colour picture of the final image

Commentary explains how the lighting set up was approached by the photographer

Photographer's personal comment on his or her picture

Distances and even sizes have been compressed and expanded: and because of the vast variety of sizes of soft boxes, reflectors, bounces and the like, we have settled on a limited range of conventionalized symbols. Sometimes, too, we have reduced the size of big bounces, just to simplify the drawing.

None of this should really matter, however. After all, no photographer works strictly according to rules and preconceptions: there is always room to move this light a little to the left or right,

to move that light closer or further away, and so forth, according to the needs of the shot. Likewise, the precise power of the individual lighting heads or (more important) the lighting ratios are not always given; but again, this is something which can be "fine tuned" by any photographer wishing to reproduce the lighting set-ups in here.

We are however confident that there is more than enough information given about every single shot to merit its inclusion in the book: as well as purely

lighting techniques, there are also all kinds of hints and tips about commercial realities, photographic practicalities, and the way of the world in general.

The book can therefore be used in a number of ways. The most basic, and perhaps the most useful for the beginner, is to study all the technical information concerning a picture which he or she particularly admires, together with the lighting diagrams, and to try to duplicate that shot as far as possible with the equipment available.

A more advanced use for the book is as a problem solver for difficulties you have already encountered: a particular technique of back lighting, say, or of creating a feeling of light and space. And, of course, it can always be used simply as a source of inspiration.

The information for each picture follows the same plan, though some individual headings may be omitted if they were irrelevant or unavailable. The photographer is credited first, then the client, together with the use for which the picture was taken. Next come the other members of the team who worked on the picture: stylists, models, art directors, whoever. Camera and lens come next, followed by film. With film, we have named brands and types, because different films have very different ways of rendering colours and tonal values. Exposure comes next: where the lighting is electronic flash, only the aperture is given, as illumination is of course independent of shutter speed. Next, the lighting equipment is briefly summarized — whether tungsten or flash, and what sort of heads — and finally there is a brief note on props and backgrounds. Often, this last will be obvious from the picture, but in other cases you may be surprised at what has been pressed into service, and how different it looks from its normal role.

The most important part of the book is however the pictures themselves. By studying these, and referring to the lighting diagrams and the text as necessary, you can work out how they were done; and showing how things are done is the brief to which the *Pro Lighting* series was created.

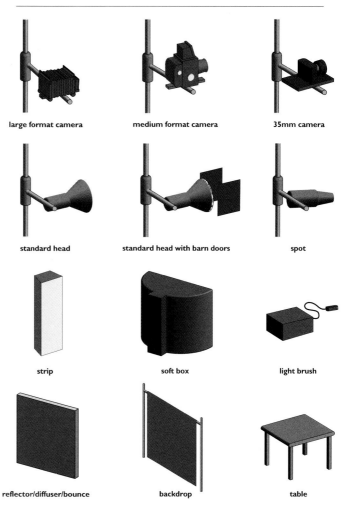

DIAGRAM KEY

The following is a key to the symbols used in the three-dimensional and plan view diagrams. All commonly used elements such as standard heads, reflectors etc., are listed. Any special or unusual elements involved will be shown on the relevant diagrams themselves.

THREE-DIMENSIONAL DIAGRAMS

large format camera   medium format camera   35mm camera

standard head   standard head with barn doors   spot

strip   soft box   light brush

reflector/diffuser/bounce   backdrop   table

PLAN VIEW DIAGRAMS

large format camera   medium format camera   35mm camera   bounce

standard head   standard head with barn doors   spot   gobo

    diffuser

    reflector

strip   soft box   light brush   backdrop   table

GLOSSARY OF LIGHTING TERMS

▼

LIGHTING, LIKE ANY OTHER CRAFT, HAS ITS OWN JARGON AND SLANG. UNFORTUNATELY, THE DIFFERENT TERMS ARE NOT VERY WELL STANDARDIZED, AND OFTEN THE SAME THING MAY BE DESCRIBED IN TWO OR MORE WAYS OR THE SAME WORD MAY BE USED TO MEAN TWO OR MORE DIFFERENT THINGS. FOR EXAMPLE, A SHEET OF BLACK CARD, WOOD, METAL OR OTHER MATERIAL WHICH IS USED TO CONTROL REFLECTIONS OR SHADOWS MAY BE CALLED A FLAG, A FRENCH FLAG, A DONKEY OR A GOBO – THOUGH SOME PEOPLE WOULD RESERVE THE TERM "GOBO" FOR A FLAG WITH HOLES IN IT, WHICH IS ALSO KNOWN AS A COOKIE. IN THIS BOOK, WE HAVE TRIED TO STANDARDIZE TERMS AS FAR AS POSSIBLE. FOR CLARITY, A GLOSSARY IS GIVEN BELOW, AND THE PREFERRED TERMS USED IN THIS BOOK ARE ASTERISKED.

Acetate
see Gel

Acrylic sheeting
Hard, shiny plastic sheeting, usually methyl methacrylate, used as a diffuser ("opal") or in a range of colours as a background.

*Barn doors
Adjustable flaps affixed to a lighting head which allow the light to be shaded from a particular part of the subject.

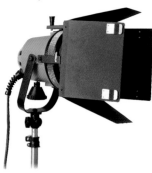

Barn doors

Boom
Extension arm allowing a light to be cantilevered out over a subject.

*Bounce
A passive reflector, typically white but also, (for example) silver or gold, from which light is bounced back onto the subject. Also used in the compound term "Black Bounce", meaning a flag used to absorb light rather than to cast a shadow.

Continuous lighting
What its name suggests: light which shines continuously instead of being a brief flash.

Contrast
see Lighting ratio

Cookie
see Gobo

*Diffuser
Translucent material used to diffuse light. Includes tracing paper, scrim, umbrellas, translucent plastics such as Perspex and Plexiglas, and more.

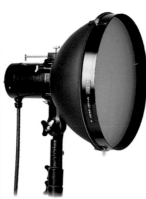

Electronic flash: standard head with parallel snoot (Strobex)

Donkey
see Gobo

Effects light
Neither key nor fill; a small light, usually a spot, used to light a particular part of the subject. A hair light on a model is an example of an effects (or "FX") light.

*Fill
Extra lights, either from a separate head or from a reflector, which "fills" the shadows and lowers the lighting ratio.

Fish fryer
A small Soft Box.

*Flag
A rigid sheet of metal, board, foam-core or other material which is used to absorb light or to create a shadow. Many flags are painted black on one side and white (or brushed silver) on the other, so that they can be used either as flags or as reflectors.

*Flat
A large Bounce, often made of a thick sheet of expanded polystyrene or foam-core (for lightness).

Foil
see Gel

French flag
see Flag

Frost
see Diffuser

*Gel
Transparent or (more rarely) translucent coloured material used to modify the colour of a light. It is an abbreviation of "gelatine (filter)", though most modern "gels" for lighting use are actually of acetate.

*Gobo
As used in this book, synonymous with "cookie": a flag with cut-outs in it, to cast interestingly-shaped shadows. Also used in projection spots.

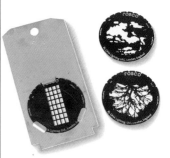

"Cookies" or "gobos" for projection spotlight (Photon Beard)

*Head
Light source, whether continuous or flash. A "standard head" is fitted with a plain reflector.

*HMI
Rapidly-pulsed and

effectively continuous light source approximating to daylight and running far cooler than tungsten. Relatively new at the time of writing, and still very expensive.

*Honeycomb

Grid of open-ended hexagonal cells, closely resembling a honeycomb. Increases directionality of

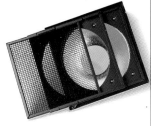

Honeycomb (Hensel)

light from any head.

Incandescent lighting

see Tungsten

Inky dinky

Small tungsten spot.

*Key or key light

The dominant or principal light, the light which casts the shadows.

Kill Spill

Large flat used to block spill.

*Light brush

Light source "piped" through fibre-optic lead. Can be used to add highlights, delete shadows and modify lighting, literally by "painting with light".

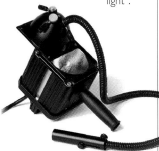

Electronic Flash: light brush "pencil" (Hensel)

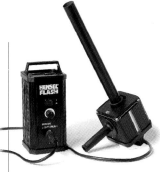

Electronic Flash: light brush "hose" (Hensel)

Lighting ratio

The ratio of the key to the fill, as measured with an incident light meter. A high lighting ratio (8:1 or above) is very contrasty, especially in colour, a low lighting ratio (4:1 or less) is flatter or softer. A 1:1 lighting ratio is completely even, all over the subject.

*Mirror

Exactly what its name suggests. The only reason for mentioning it here is that reflectors are rarely mirrors, because mirrors create "hot spots" while reflectors diffuse light. Mirrors (especially small shaving mirrors) are however widely used, almost in the same way as effects lights.

Northlight

see Soft Box

Perspex

Brand name for acrylic sheeting.

Plexiglas

Brand name for acrylic sheeting.

*Projection spot

Flash or tungsten head with projection optics for casting a clear image of a gobo or cookie. Used to create textured lighting effects and shadows.

*Reflector

Either a dish-shaped surround to a light, or a bounce.

*Scrim

Heat-resistant fabric

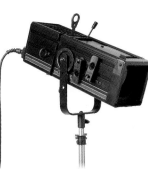

Electronic Flash: projection spotlight (Strobex)

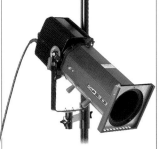

Tungsten Projection spotlight (Photon Beard)

diffuser, used to soften lighting.

*Snoot

Conical restrictor, fitting over a lighting head. The light can only escape from the small hole in the end, and is

therefore very directional.

*Soft box

Large, diffuse light source made by shining a light

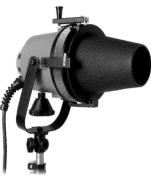

Tungsten spot with conical snoot (Photon Beard)

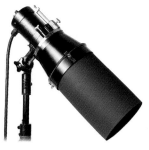

Electronic Flash: standard head with parallel snoot (Strobex)

through one or two layers of diffuser. Soft boxes come in all kinds of shapes

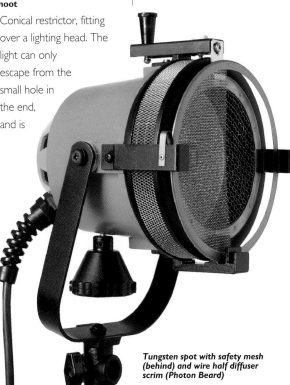

Tungsten spot with safety mesh (behind) and wire half diffuser scrim (Photon Beard)

Electronic flash: standard head with large reflector and diffuser (Strobex)

and sizes, from about 30×30cm to 120×180cm and larger. Some soft boxes are rigid; others are made of fabric stiffened with poles resembling fibreglass fishing rods. Also known as a northlight or a windowlight, though these can also be created by shining standard heads through large (120×180cm or larger) diffusers.

*Spill

Light from any source which ends up other than on the subject at which it is pointed. Spill may be used to provide fill, or to light backgrounds, or it may be controlled with flags, barn doors, gobos etc.

*Spot

Directional light source. Normally refers to a light using a focusing system

with reflectors or lenses or both, a "focusing spot", but also loosely used as a reflector head rendered more directional with a honeycomb.

*Strip or strip light

Lighting head, usually flash, which is much longer than it is wide.

Electronic flash: strip light with removable barn doors (Strobex)

Strobe

Electronic flash. Strictly, a "strobe" is a stroboscope or rapidly repeating light source, though it is also the name of a leading manufacturer.

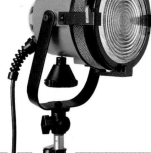

Tungsten spot with removable Fresnel lens. The knob at the bottom varies the width of the beam (Photon Beard)

Strobex, formerly Strobe Equipment.

Swimming pool

A very large Soft Box.

*Tungsten

Incandescent lighting. Photographic tungsten

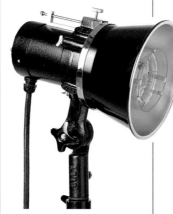

Electronic flash: standard head with standard reflector (Strobex)

lighting runs at 3200°K or 3400°K, as compared with domestic lamps which run at 2400°K to 2800°K or thereabouts.

*Umbrella

Exactly what its name suggests; used for modifying light.

Umbrellas may be used as reflectors (light shining into the umbrella) or diffusers (light shining through the umbrella). The cheapest way of creating a large, soft light source.

Windowlight

Apart from the obvious meaning of light through a window, or of light shone through a diffuser to look as if it is coming through a window, this is another name for a soft box.

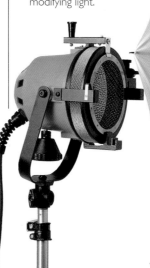

Tungsten spot with shoot-through umbrella (Photon Beard)

PORTRAITS

▼

Until the invention of photography, the "likeness" was the preserve of the very rich. Skilled painters and sculptors have always been rare, and their work takes a long time, which translates into high costs.

Traditionally, portraits were intended to be as flattering as possible. We do not really know what (say) Queen Elizabeth looked like. We may assume that her famous portraits were passing likenesses, but it is less certain that we would recognize her from them if we were to see her in the street, dressed perhaps in jeans and a T-shirt instead of the magnificent court dresses, stiff with jewels, in which she was usually represented.

The tradition of flattery and aggrandizement lasted well beyond the invention of photography, too. Think of Lenin. The Socialist Realist style in which his portraits and statues were created makes him look far more heroic than most of his photographs; but we remember him from his iconic representations, not from his "likenesses."

Even where realistic portraits are readily available, there is still an inevitable tendency to accept the iconic over the homely or naturalistic: think, for example, of the countless portraits of Churchill which exist, and of the relatively few which appear again and again in the press and which have achieved iconic status partly as a result of their inherent qualities, and partly through sheer repetition.

To this day, therefore, the portrait lends itself remarkably well to deconstruction. For example, it may be a symbol of The Business Leader, The Family Man, The Professor, The Affluent Consumer, The Sex Goddess. In this sense, it is to some extent independent of its subject. He or she is merely a tool that is used to illustrate a theme or to sell a product (an airline ticket, a brand of beer) or a concept (the American way of life, success in academia, European café society).

In another context a portrait may be a "likeness" of a particular person – but the camera always lies. Through one photographer's lens, the subject is relaxed, cheerful. Through another's he or she is stern, cold, harsh.

In yet a third context the image may transcend both personality and symbol: we see an arrangement of curves and textures and lines which is in itself beautiful.

This leads us to the question of why photographers take portraits. Some do it just for money, of course. But even the most commercial of portrait photographers must have a reason to photograph people instead of something else. And many photographers sincerely want to capture a likeness which is more than skin deep; they want to "get under the skin" of their subject, to make a psychological interpretation.

The circularity of the process then becomes apparent: the portrait is as much a psychological interpretation of the photographer as of the person photographed. There are cruel photographers and kind photographers, gentle photographers and harsh photographers, light-hearted photographers and very serious photographers. The photographer takes portraits for one set of reasons, and the subject may sit for them for an entirely different set of reasons, and the picture is the only place where they meet.

If you can bear to do so without feeling too self-conscious or pretentious, you might therefore do well to ask yourself why you take pictures. What do you want to say with the pictures? Who do you want to see them? What do you want them to say when they see the pictures?

This can affect your technical style as well as your aesthetics. Gritty black and white creates one image; flawless colour creates another. A small print may be intimate, or merely insignificant; a big print can be impressive, or imposing, or just plain vulgar.

STUDIOS AND CONTEXTS

The choice between a studio portrait and a portrait of the subject in a wider context – the so-called "environmental" or location portrait – is a matter of personal styles; and besides, there are no real distinctions between the two. Some traditionally minded portrait photographers maintain built sets in which to photograph their sitters: the book-lined library is a well-established favourite, and the boudoir has apparently done well for some. Equally, a location may be so bare that it supplies little more context than a roll of background paper.

Even so, the photographer must consider which approach to take. Some take their lead from Richard Avedon and photograph their subjects against a featureless white background; others like to show people in settings which are crowded almost to the point of surrealism. There are also many options in between. Arguably, though, the photographer must rely more on psychological interpretation when the background is minimal; in a more complex environment, whether a built set or a location, he or she is more concerned with the *gestalt*, the whole.

Remember, too, that few people are totally one-dimensional and consistent: they exist in different milieus, and by learning a little more about them, you may be able to place them in a setting with which they, or you, or both, are more at ease. The lawyer, for example, may be a secret wind-surfer; the accountant may ride a motorcycle. If you take this route, however, remember that there can be a gap between how people want to see themselves, and how they are going to look convincing. Some accountants are never going to look like bad-ass bikers, in the same way that some Hell's Angels are never going to look like accountants. They may not realise the discrepancy — there is

enough of a market in fantasy portraits to prove this — but the question is, are you comfortable taking that sort of picture?

CLOTHES, PROPS AND MAKE-UP

As with the choice between the bare background and the crowded environment, so the photographer (and the sitter) must choose between the casual picture taken in everyday clothes and the formal portrait, the sort of thing our ancestors might have characterized as Sunday Best. Again, there is a wide range of options in between, including the pseudo-informal portrait (where the casual jeans are carefully chosen and freshly washed, the hair done, the setting spruced up for the occasion) and the deliberately subversive juxtaposition: in the novel *Bedazzled*, for example, the Devil must always wear red socks and old sneakers, regardless of how elegantly he may otherwise be dressed.

If the photographer leans towards the formal or the pseudo-informal, or if the portrait is to be used for advertising or some other public purpose, then it may well be worth calling on the services of professional make-up artists and hairdressers and even professional clothing advisers and prop-finders.

A specialist case is the makeover portrait, where all the stops are pulled out to transform an average (or even below-average) young woman into a passing facsimile of a Hollywood star from the golden days of film stills. Today, this is normally achieved with make-up and lighting (and lashings of soft focus) rather than with the kind of heavy airbrush retouching which was

the norm in the 1930s, 1940s and 1950s. This is a highly specialised form of portraiture, but it is also one which can be great fun for all concerned as well as being very lucrative.

Working on a more modest scale, the photographer must at least be aware of what make-up, hair, and careful choice of clothes and props can do, and it is a good idea whenever possible to talk through a portrait with the subject before they come to the studio to be photographed. Ask them what they intend to wear, what sort of image they want to project – and advise them to bring with them a favourite and characteristic personal possession. Think of your friends and their eccentricities and mannerisms: the man who wears a monocle, the girl who is forever playing with a heavy gold bangle. Everyone has these personal foibles; it is the job of the paid portraitist to capture them.

CAMERAS AND FILM FOR PORTRAITS

The camera of choice for most portraitists is a medium-format reflex, typically used with a longer-than-standard lens; in fact, 150mm and 180mm lenses on medium-format cameras are often known as "portrait" lenses. Medium formats allow better sharpness, smoother gradation and less grain than 35mm, but are still sufficiently rapid-handling to allow a degree of spontaneity. They are also significantly cheaper to run than large-format cameras. The modern tendency is in any case to shoot a number of similar portraits – typically a roll or two of 120, between 10 and 30 images – and then to select the best.

Another reason why rollfilm is so popular among High Street portrait photographers is that special colour negative portrait films in this format are offered by a number of manufacturers. They are optimized for skin tones, and typically have a lower contrast than standard colour print films.

There is also a place for 35mm in portraiture, often with very long lenses, and surprisingly often with Polaroid materials, which give effects quite unlike those obtainable with anything else.

LIGHTING EQUIPMENT FOR PORTRAITS

As in most other branches of photography, it is possible to make generalizations about portrait lighting set-ups. The first and most important generalization, which immediately distinguishes the skilled portrait photographer from the unskilled, is that the background is separately lit from the subject. This allows the background to be lightened or darkened (or graded) independently of the subject. In order to do this, there must be a fair amount of space between the subject and the background: at the very least 1.5m (5ft) and preferably 2 or even 3m (6½ or 10ft).

After this, it is surprising how many photographers use a single light to one side of the camera plus a reflector on the other side to provide a fill. The intellectual argument in favour of a single light is that this is what we have evolved to expect: there is one sun in the sky, and the light from the cave-mouth comes from one direction only. If more than one light is used, it should therefore be used with good reason – and there

are plenty of good reasons shown in this book. Hair lights are a familiar example, but they are only one of many kinds of (usually highly directional) effects lights which are used to draw attention to a particular feature.

Another reason to use extra lights (or complex multiple reflectors) is to create a very even overall light, which can be particularly flattering to women and children. As a general though far from unbreakable rule, highly directional lighting is more widely used for men, and more diffuse and even lighting for women and children.

THE TEAM

Many portrait photographers work alone, though it is often useful to have an assistant to move the lights so that the photographer can judge the effects without having to leave the camera position. It is also highly desirable to have remote controls for the lights so that they can be switched on or off, or turned up or down, from the camera position.

In advertising and publicity photography, and in the higher reaches of corporate portraiture, at least one assistant is all but essential and there is likely to be a need for specialist make-up artists, etc, as mentioned above.

THE PORTRAIT SESSION

Sometimes a portrait session goes as if by magic. There is an immediate rapport between the photographer and the subject, and the pictures just go on getting better. Sitter and photographer spark ideas off one another, and both are sorry when they have to stop.

At the other extreme, the sitter is in a hurry and does not particularly want to be photographed anyway. As quickly as possible, the portraitist has to put the sitter at ease, get the picture, and get out.

Either way, the preparation is the same. The photographer must already have a pretty clear idea of how the session is going to be organized: where the lights are going to be, what the pose and props will be, and how the picture will be framed. Setting up should be as fast as possible, and there should be little fiddling about with equipment or exposure readings. All of this is much easier in the studio, of course.

The photographer should if possible know something about the sitter in advance: easy conversation can make all the difference between establishing a rapport with the subject (which almost always shows in a picture) and a formal, lifeless portrait. Some photographers have a natural gift for this; others do not. Some subjects like to see Polaroids; others, particularly those who are full of their own importance, may simply want you out as soon as possible.

Beyond this, it is down to you. Portraits are perhaps the most idiosyncratic branch of photography – unless that prize is taken by reportage, which often consists of portraits under another name – and the personality of the photographer can be paramount. There are at least as many ways of seeing as there are photographers and a good number of those ways of seeing are represented in this book. Enjoy it.

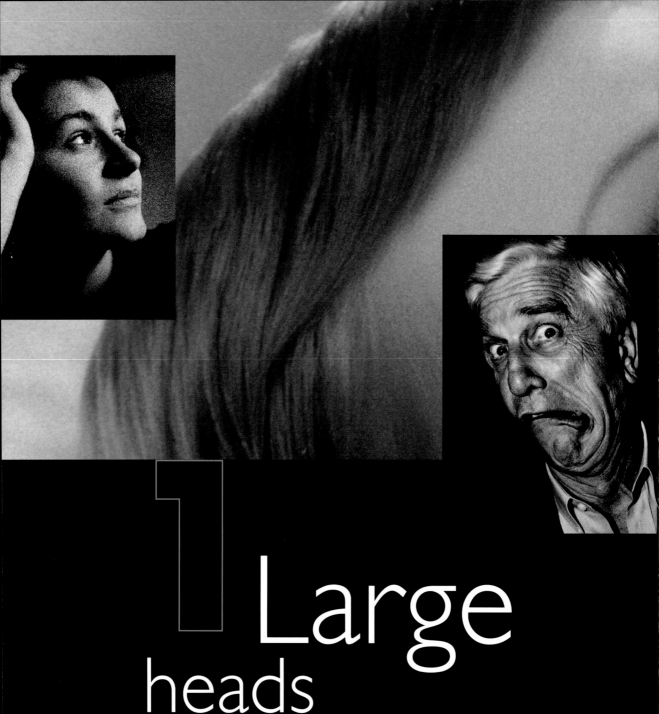

1 Large
heads

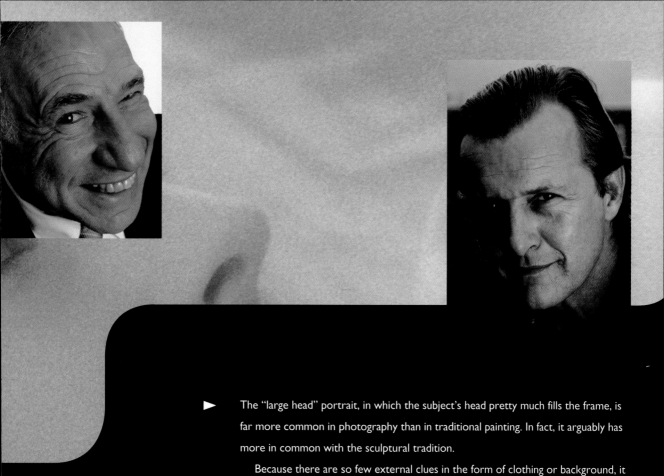

The "large head" portrait, in which the subject's head pretty much fills the frame, is far more common in photography than in traditional painting. In fact, it arguably has more in common with the sculptural tradition.

Because there are so few external clues in the form of clothing or background, it

JUSTINE

▼

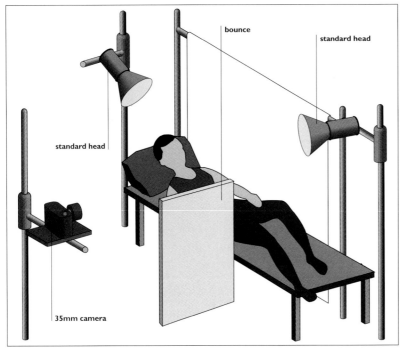

Photographer: **Marc Joye**

Use: **Self-promotional**

Model: **Justine**

Camera: **35mm**

Lens: **150mm, light amber filter**

Film: **Kodak High Speed infrared**

Exposure: **f/11**

Lighting: **Electronic flash: 2 heads**

Props and set: **White background**

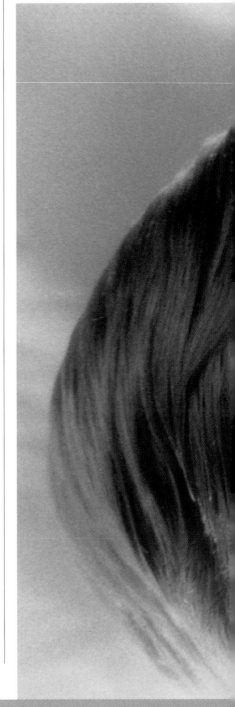

THIS PORTRAIT OWES AS MUCH TO THE SOFT, FLARY, GRAINY NATURE OF KODAK'S HIGH SPEED INFRARED FILM AS TO THE LIGHTING, WHICH IS A STRAIGHTFORWARD DOUBLE BACK LIGHT WITH A BOUNCE TO CAMERA RIGHT.

The same thing – choice of film – explains the very high-key effect: over-exposure, together with the IR sensitization of the film, lightens the hair and the eyes. It is interesting that the photographer has chosen weak filtration, so as to retain the normal sensitization of the film as well as the IR sensitization. With the more usual deep red filtration, an unpleasantly dead and corpse-like appearance often results: this is periodically exploited for its shock value by rock photographers, who imagine that they are being novel and daring rather than tired and hackneyed.

It is worth noting that the IR output of flash tubes varies widely, so any attempt to use flash with IR should be preceded with a check of the emission spectrum of the flash equipment in use.

Photographer's comment:

I like to photograph on infrared film, where the warmth of the body contributes to the image. Justine has very dark eyes, but in this way they become light and she looks very different from usual.

► The sensitization of IR films varies widely, from Kodak's High Speed infrared (sensitized beyond 900nm) to Konica and Ilford materials sensitized to 750nm and 740nm respectively

► Full (deep red) IR filtration creates effects very different from weaker or no filtration

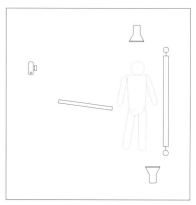

Plan View

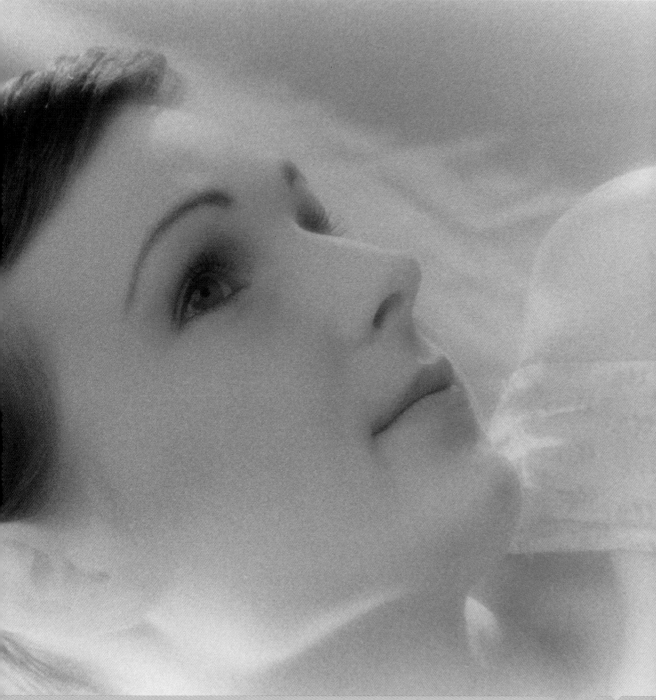

Photographer: **Rudi Mühlbauer**

Use: **Self-promotional**

Model: **Michaela**

Camera: **35mm**

Lens: **50mm**

Film: **Kodak TMZ at EI 3200**

Exposure: **1/60 second at f/2.8**

Lighting: **Tungsten: single diffused lamp**

Props and set: **White wall as background**

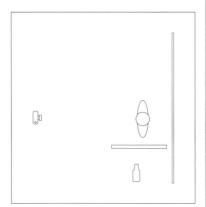

Plan View

▼

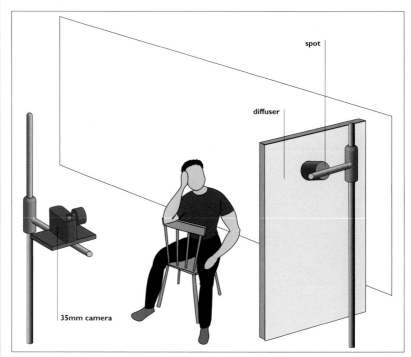

DIFFUSED BUT DIRECTIONAL LIGHT CAN BE EXTREMELY EFFECTIVE AND NATURAL-LOOKING. THE MAIN PROBLEMS FOR THE PHOTOGRAPHER LIE IN GETTING ENOUGH LIGHT IN THE FIRST PLACE, AND IN MAKING A BIG ENOUGH DIFFUSER.

Rudi Mühlbauer solved the first problem in two ways: by using a very powerful single light source – 1000 Watts is as powerful a light as many photographers will have access to – and by using a very fast film, Kodak's TMZ, rated at EI 3200. Although TMZ is an ISO 1000 film which can deliver shadow detail at up to EI 1600 or so, many photographers push it to EI 3200, EI 6400, EI 12,500 and even EI 25,000, both for speed alone and for the aesthetic effects of the grain.

As for making a big diffuser – this one was 2m (6½ft) square – the easiest solution is to buy something like a Scrim Jim, which is a large metal frame with interchangeable fabric diffusers and reflectors. Other possibilities include tracing paper or even bedsheets; nylon sheets are ideal.

► *Ultra-fast, grainy films are not just attractive in their own right: they also have the advantage that they can be used with comparatively low-powered or distant light sources, including photoflood bulbs of modest wattage*

► *Very large, diffuse light sources can be achieved by diffusion or by bouncing light off a reflector*

Photographer's comment:

I was attempting to imitate soft, morning light in the studio, with just one lamp.

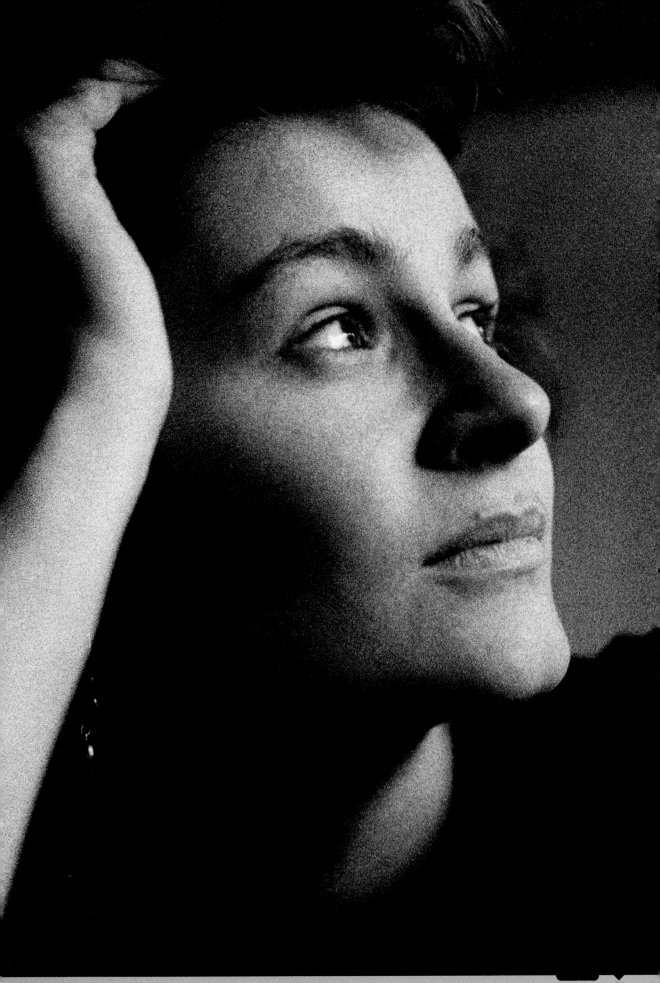

Photographer: **Ben Lagunas & Alex Kuri**

Client: **Michell Ritz**

Use: **Editorial**

Model: **Zarina**

Assistants: **Isak de Ita, George Jacob**

Art director: **Many Boy**

Camera: **4x5in**

Lens: **300mm**

Film: **Kodak Ektachrome EPP 100**

Exposure: **f/11**

Lighting: **Electronic flash: 7 heads**

Props and set: **White background**

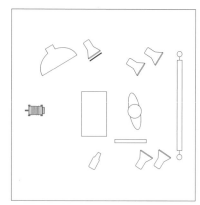

Plan View

▼

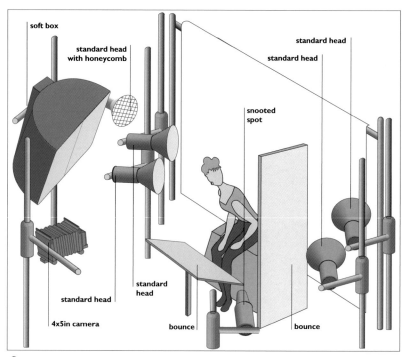

SEVEN LIGHT SOURCES WOULD NORMALLY BE A RECIPE FOR DISASTER IN A PORTRAIT — UNLESS YOU KNEW WHAT YOU WERE DOING, AS BEN LAGUNAS AND ALEX KURI PLAINLY DID. IN THIS CASE, FOUR OF THE LIGHT SOURCES ARE STANDARD HEADS USED TO "BURN OUT" THE BACKGROUND FOR A HIGH-KEY EFFECT.

After that, everything is easier to understand. The key is the snooted spot, high (2m/6½ft off the ground) and to camera right. A standard head with a honeycomb provides some fill from camera left, but (more importantly) adds highlights to the model's hair. A purple gel on this head also creates the unusual colour effects which are "washed out" on the right of the picture by the stronger key light. A (non-filtered) soft box, also to camera left, further softens the contrast.

On a 4x5in, a 300mm lens is ideal for portraits: it equates roughly to 100mm on 35mm and 150mm on 6x6cm. Although f/11 is a relatively small aperture on smaller formats, on a 4x5in format with a long lens it allows highly selective focus.

► *High-key backgrounds normally require a very great deal of light. The alternative is to light the subject in the foreground relatively weakly, and give a longer exposure (with tungsten), use a wider aperture, or use a faster film*

► *Using gels to distort colours is very much a matter of personal taste and vision — and a picture which one person loves, another may hate*

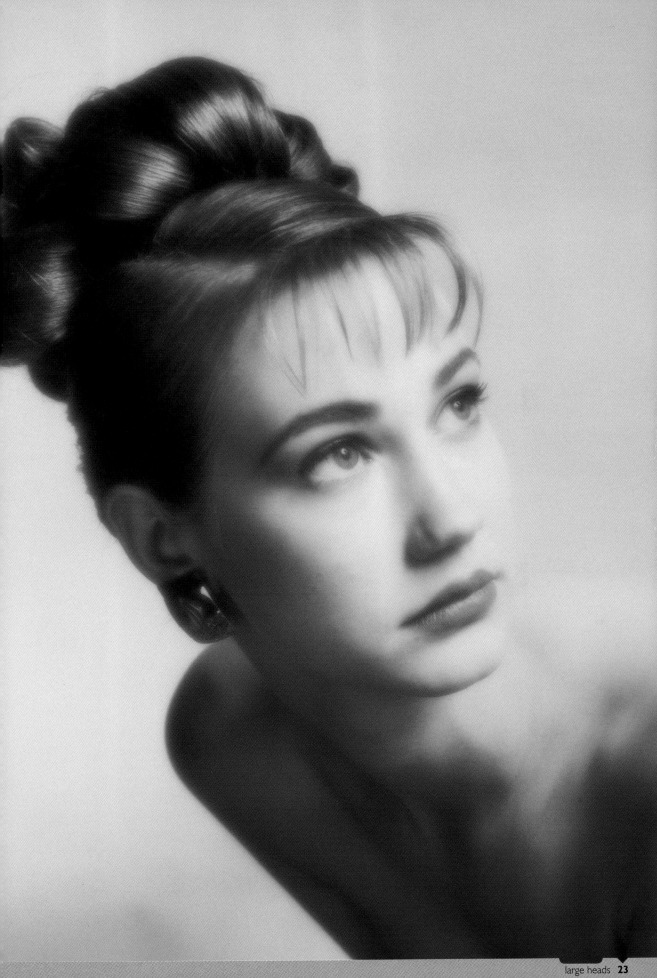

Photographer: **Dolors Porredon**

Client: **Studio**

Use: **Poster**

Camera: **6x6cm**

Lens: **150mm**

Film: **Kodak Vericolor 2**

Exposure: **f/5.6**

Lighting: **Flash: 2 heads**

Props and set: **Painted backdrop**

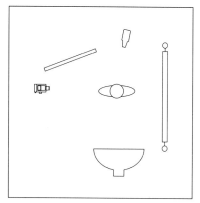

Plan View

▼

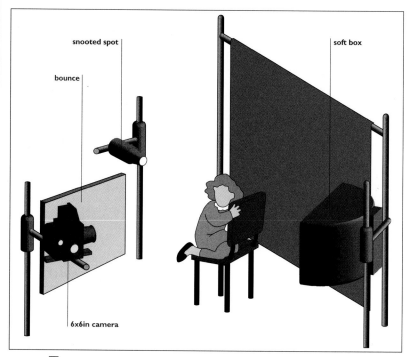

snooted spot

soft box

bounce

6x6in camera

THE FACE, THE POSE, THE COLOURS: ALL ARE REMINISCENT OF A VICTORIAN CHROMOLITHOGRAPH. THE EFFECT IS ACHIEVED IN LARGE MEASURE BY CAREFUL CONTROL OF THE LIGHTING RATIO, WHILE RETAINING AS MUCH CHIAROSCURO AS POSSIBLE.

There is a snooted spot to camera left, fairly close to the child's face and very slightly backlighting her. The key light, to camera right, is a 60x80cm (2x3ft) soft box. This is set to give quite a close lighting ratio, but because it is diffuse and the key light is highly directional, the impression of modelling is very clear: modelling is all the more clear, of course, because of the very careful angling of these two lights.

A white reflector to camera left, just out of shot, provides a little more fill to the front of the face but (more importantly) also creates the catch-lights in the eyes. They would not be there otherwise: the key is a back light, and the fill is shaded from both eyes.

► Catch-lights in the eyes are not essential, but sometimes a picture which is lacking them will look curiously dead

► Traditional portraitists touched out all but a single catchlight. Today, multiple catchlights are acceptable if they are not too obtrusive

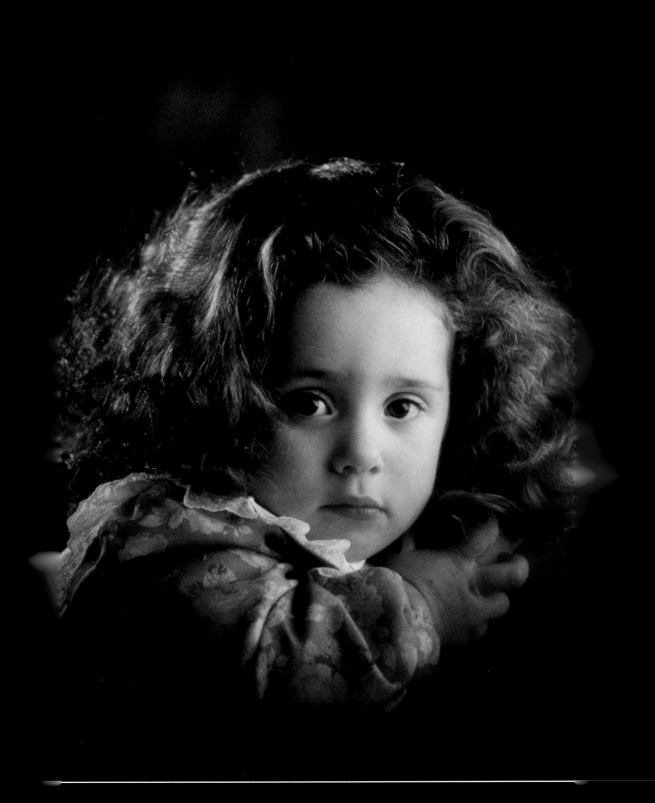

BUSINESS WOMAN/ MICHELLE

▼

Photographer: **Harry Lomax**

Use: **Library and model's portfolio**

Model: **Michelle**

Camera: **4x5in**

Lens: **210mm**

Film: **Fuji RDP ISO 100**

Exposure: **f/16**

Lighting: **Flash: 2 umbrellas**

Props and set: **Black velvet background**

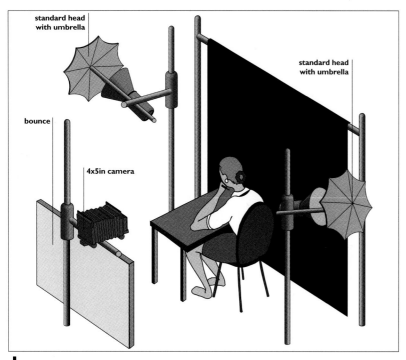

standard head with umbrella

standard head with umbrella

bounce

4x5in camera

LIBRARY SHOTS LIKE THIS ARE OFTEN MORE IN DEMAND (AND FACE LESS COMPETITION) THAN CONVENTIONAL PICTURES OF PRETTY GIRLS. THEY HAVE TO BE CAREFULLY THOUGHT OUT, THEN CAREFULLY SET UP, AND AFTER A WHILE THEY WILL BEGIN TO DATE; BUT DURING THEIR LIFE, THEY CAN DO VERY WELL.

The lighting must be at once dramatic enough to attract attention, but sufficiently unobtrusive not to look inappropriate. Harry Lomax used two umbrellas. The key light was about 3m (10ft) to camera left, above the model's eye-line and slightly back lighting her. The secondary light was to camera right, at a similar distance and height, and set to half the power of the first.

Just below the camera, a 120cm (47in) square bounce provided fill: the bounce and the camera were about 150cm (5ft) from the model, with the camera below the model's eye-line in order to emphasize her height and importance. Looking up at a subject makes them look important, in the same way that looking down emphasizes vulnerability or even inferiority.

► Models' portfolio shots are an excellent opportunity for both models and photographers seeking stock (library) material, and both parties should be prepared to spend as much time and money on them as is necessary to get a first-class result

► Models and photographers should interview one another carefully, to learn one anothers' expectations, experience, and budget

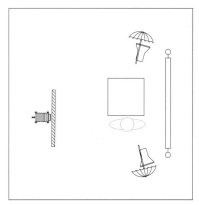

Plan View

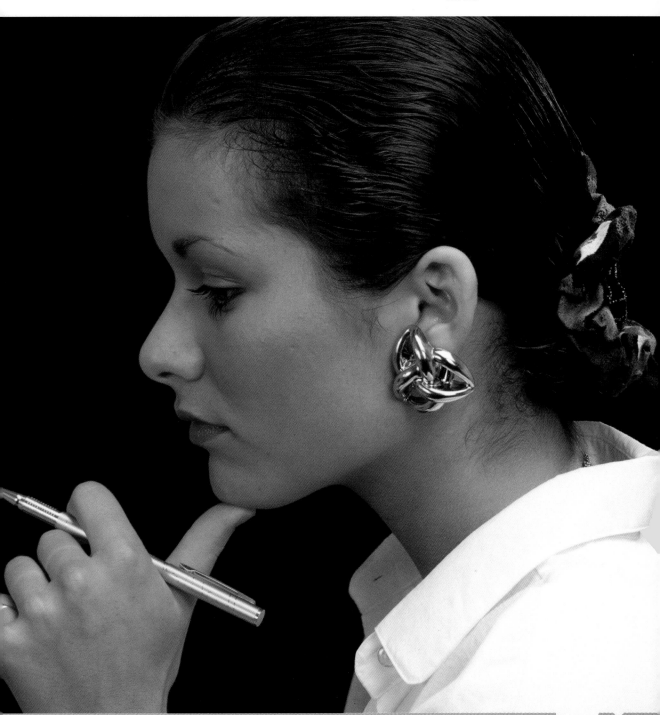

Photographer: **Alan Sheldon**

Client: **Virgin Vision**

Use: **Publicity**

Art director: **Carey Bayley**

Camera: **645**

Lens: **150mm**

Film: **Fujichrome RDP ISO 100**

Exposure: **1/30 second at f/11**

Lighting: **Mixed: see text**

Props and set: **Location**

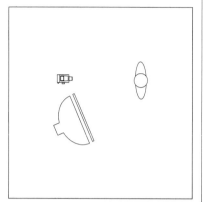

Plan View

R U T G E R   H A U E R

▼

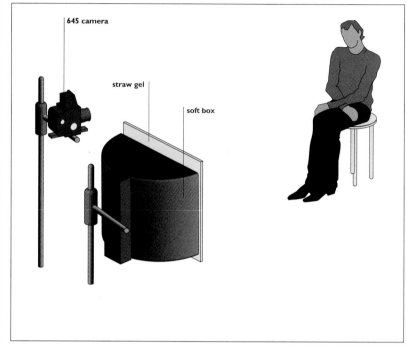

645 camera

straw gel

soft box

THIS IS A CLASSIC "FAKE SETTING-SUN" PICTURE. IF YOU TRY TO SHOOT BY THE REAL LIGHT OF THE SETTING SUN, YOU RUN INTO VERY LONG EXPOSURES AND EVEN MORE REDNESS THAN YOU WANT — AND YOU HAVE ONLY A FEW SECONDS TO SHOOT ANYWAY.

The technique, therefore, is to meter for the available light; stop down at least one stop, and preferably two, for the *nuit américain* look; then balance your additional light to suit this, still underexposing very slightly in order to get the dark, end-of-the-day look.

The additional light in this case is a surprisingly large soft box, about 80×100cm (30×40in) with a straw gel to simulate the setting sun; it is quite a long way away from the subject, so that the shape of the catch-lights in the eyes is not a give-away.

► *Daylight encompasses quite a wide range of colours: the setting sun is actually redder than tungsten lighting*

► *Over-lighting the foreground when using fill-flash is always a risk; as this shot shows, slight underexposure looks much more natural*

► *Keep light sources far enough away so that they do not reflect as unnaturally-shaped catch-lights in "sunlit" shots*

Photographer's comment:

I used always to light from the left, but when I lit Rutger Hauer from the left, he looked like David Hamilton! Since then, I have found that it is a good general rule to light a man from the same side that he parts his hair.

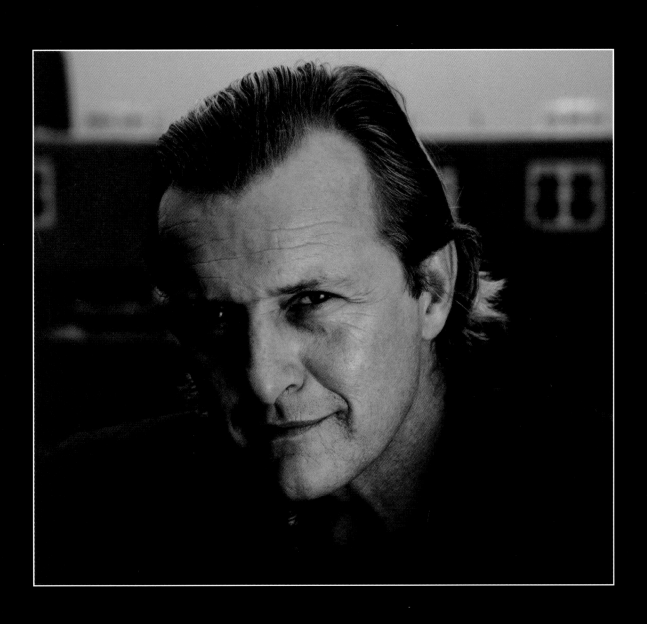

Photographer: **Alan Sheldon**

Client: **Planet Hollywood**

Use: **Display and PR**

Camera: **6x7cm**

Lens: **165mm**

Film: **Kodak Tri-X Pan at EI 320**

Exposure: **f/11**

Lighting: **On-camera flash**

Props and set: **Location**

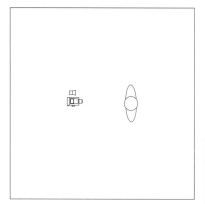

Plan View

► *"Old-technology" films like Tri-X and Ilford HP5 Plus are much more forgiving of over- and underexposure than more modern films*

► *A secret of using on-camera flash is an uncluttered background – though this can sometimes be improved at the printing stage*

▼

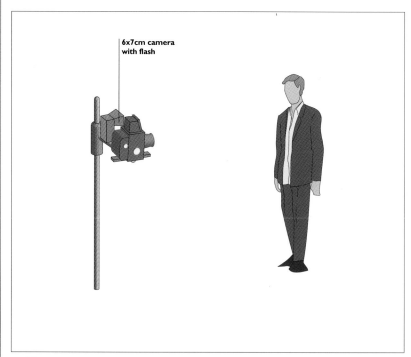

6x7cm camera with flash

THIS WAS SHOT AS PART OF THE PUBLICITY MATERIAL FOR *NAKED GUN 33⅓* AT PLANET HOLLYWOOD. THE ONLY LIGHT WAS AN ON-CAMERA METZ 45, MOUNTED TO THE LEFT OF THE CAMERA – BUT MANY PHOTOGRAPHERS COULD NOT BETTER THIS IN THE STUDIO.

The most important thing is the dead black background, achieved partly by shooting at a very modest aperture and partly by looking very carefully through the viewfinder. A close second to this is the superb tonality of Tri-X under this sort of condition: compare this with the photograph of Mel Brooks by the same photographer, using the same film but under controlled conditions, on page 55. The third thing which gives this picture its magic is the use of the 6x7cm format: a 35mm camera may be more immediate, but it can never deliver the sort of tonality of a larger format. On the other hand, in the photographer's words, the 6x7 Pentax is hell to focus in poor light.

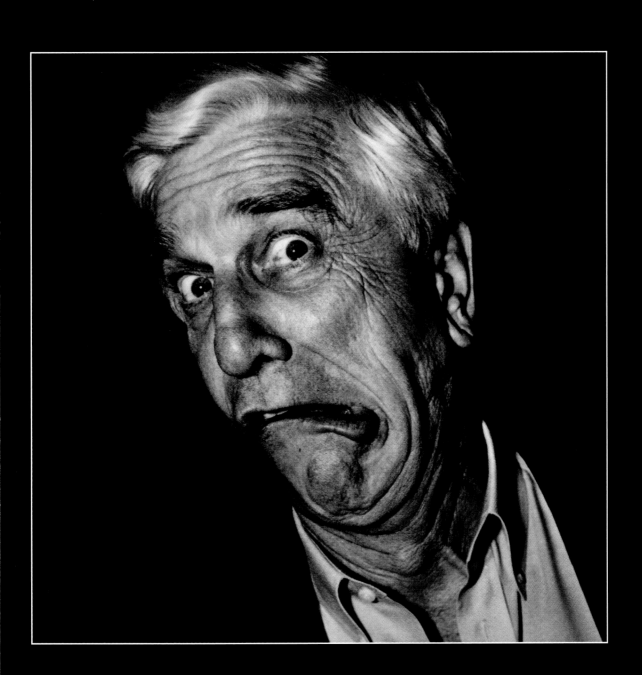

Photographer: **Alan Sheldon**

Client: **20th Century Fox**

Use: **Press/publicity**

Camera: **645**

Lens: **80mm**

Film: **Fuji RDP ISO 100**

Exposure: **1/60 second at f/8**

Lighting: **Electronic flash: 3 heads**

Props and set: **White background paper**

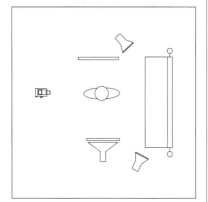

Plan View

MEL BROOKS

▼

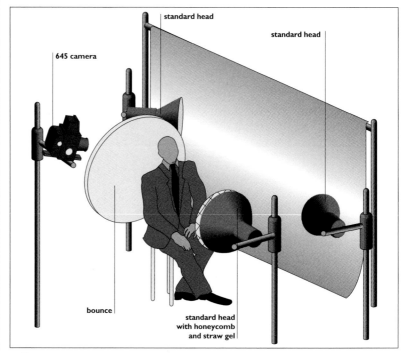

ALTHOUGH AN 80MM LENS IS NOT NORMALLY REGARDED AS IDEAL FOR PORTRAITURE ON 6X4.5CM — SOMETHING LIKE 150MM IS MORE USUAL — THE ADVANTAGE OF AN 80MM IS THAT, IF IT IS USED PROPERLY, IT CAN CONVEY TREMENDOUS IMMEDIACY AND INTIMACY.

The lighting on Mel Brooks was a single standard head with a large, square reflector – about 30cm (12in) square – with a medium honeycomb. It was to camera right, about on a level with the subject's eye-line and not quite at right angles to the line of sight. The effect is more directional than a soft box, but less directional than a spot. A straw gel warmed the light slightly to give a sunnier complexion.

A Lastolite reflector to camera left, just out of shot, provided a modest amount of fill on the right side of Mel Brooks's face. Two more lights, both with standard reflectors, lit the background to a clear, bright white.

► *For informal portraits, quite modest focal lengths can be appropriate: 80mm on 645 equates roughly to 50mm on 35mm or 180mm on 4x5in*

► *Large reflectors create an effect between standard reflectors and soft boxes*

Photographer's comment:

Mel Brooks had apparently told several people that he wasn't going to have pictures made; but fortunately I knew his manager, and I was able to prevail upon him that way.

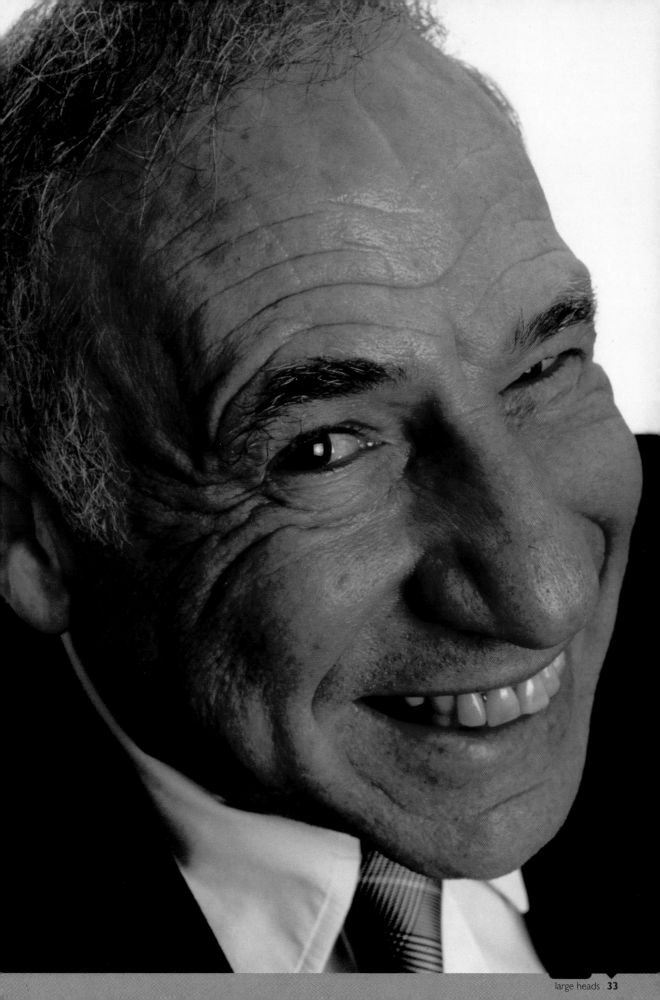

Photographer: **Alan Sheldon**

Client: **United International Pictures**

Use: **Press and internal publicity**

Camera: **645**

Lens: **150mm**

Film: **Kodak Tri-X Pan rated at EI 200**

Exposure: **f/3.5**

Lighting: **Electronic flash: 2 heads**

Props and set: **White background**

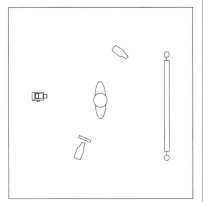

Plan View

▼

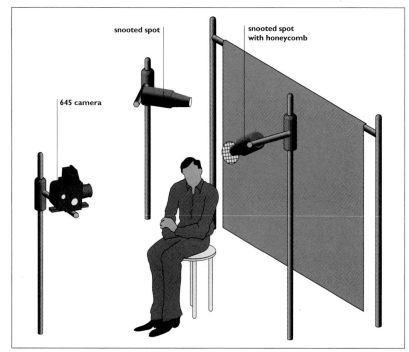

AT FIRST GLANCE – AND ON CLOSER EXAMINATION, FOR THAT MATTER – THIS LOOKS VERY LIKE A CLASSIC HOLLYWOOD PORTRAIT WITH TRADITIONALLY COMPLEX LIGHTING. IN FACT, THERE IS ONLY A SINGLE LIGHT ON MR CORMAN, WITH ANOTHER ON THE BACKGROUND.

The key light is a single standard head, tightly snooted and honeycombed, from camera right. It is very slightly in front of the subject's eye-line, and rather above it: look at the shadow of the nose. The other light is shaped to the background, which also provides a modest amount of spill to act as fill: look at the reflections on the hair behind the right ear. In practice, though, a good deal depended on manipulation of the print. The printer, Volker Wolf, darkened down the "hot" forehead considerably; as the photographer said, if he had had any powder, he could have held the forehead with far less burning in, but he didn't have a make-up person on the shoot. The edges of the print have also been darkened appreciably in printing, and the print was toned.

► *Shooting at full aperture has reproduced the shallow depth of field which characterizes traditional Hollywood portraits*

► *Skilled printing can add still more to a dramatic portrait*

Photographer's comment:

In a picture like this, where depth of field is crucial, do not use the microprism centre of the screen and then recompose. Instead, check the sharpness of the eyes on the ground glass.

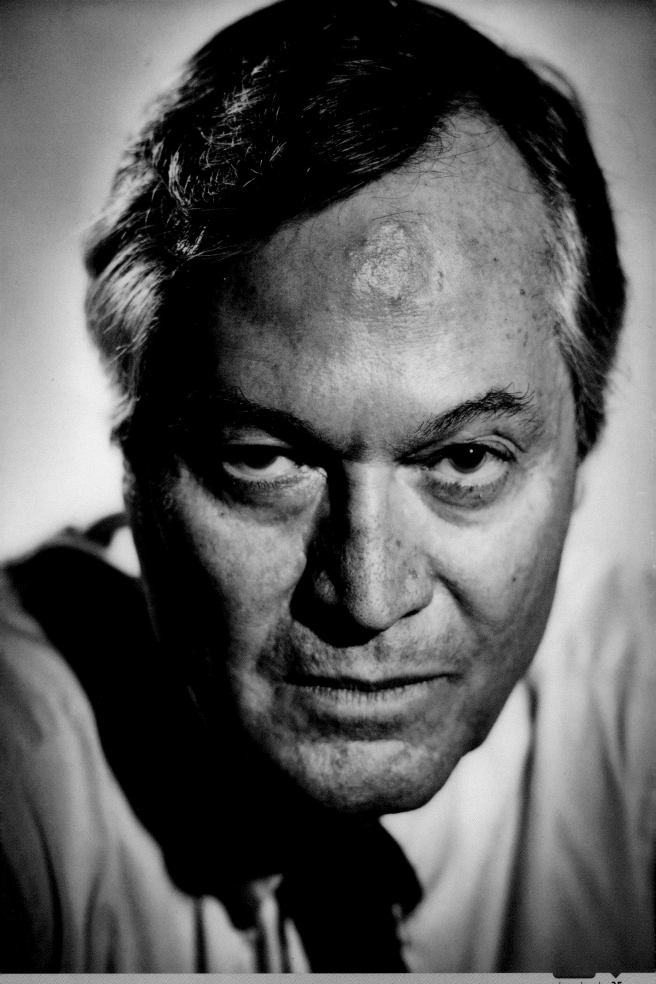

Photographer: **Frank P. Wartenberg**

Use: **Portfolio**

Camera: **35mm**

Lens: **105mm**

Film: **Kodak EPR processed as C41**

Exposure: **Not recorded**

Lighting: **Daylight plus reflectors**

Props and set: **Location**

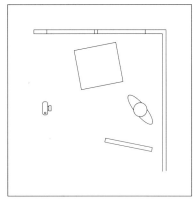

Plan View

WOMAN WITH HAIR OVER FACE

▼

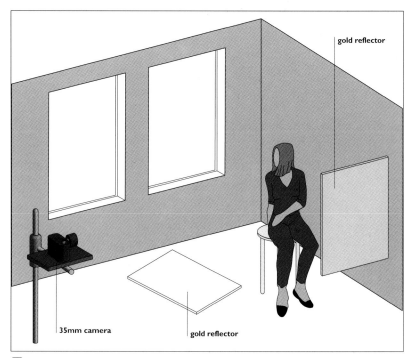

gold reflector

35mm camera

gold reflector

THE PHOTOGRAPHER SUMS UP THE LOCATION VERY WELL: "A FLAT WITH TWO BIG WINDOWS AND A DOOR TO A BALCONY." ONE CAN WELL IMAGINE HOW THE LIGHT MIGHT BE ATTRACTIVE; BUT THIS IS FAR FROM A STRAIGHTFORWARD SHOT.

First, the light was modified with the help of two gold reflectors: one on the floor, between the model and the window, and one on the far side of the model from the window. Full gold reflectors can have a remarkably warming effect, almost enough to account for the colour without anything further. In addition, though, the transparency film was cross-processed in C41 chemicals to give a negative which was used to make the final image. This gives a soft, grainy effect, often with considerable distortions of colour and contrast. A more naturalistic picture might not have worked if cross-processed; but this creates a remarkably dreamy effect.

► *"Full gold" reflectors must be used with discretion, except when colour distortion is deliberately sought*

► *Cross-processing E6 (transparency) films in C41 (negative) chemistry gives surprisingly widely varying results with different films*

► *Long lenses and wide apertures are a traditional combination for portraits but also lend themselves to non-traditional images*

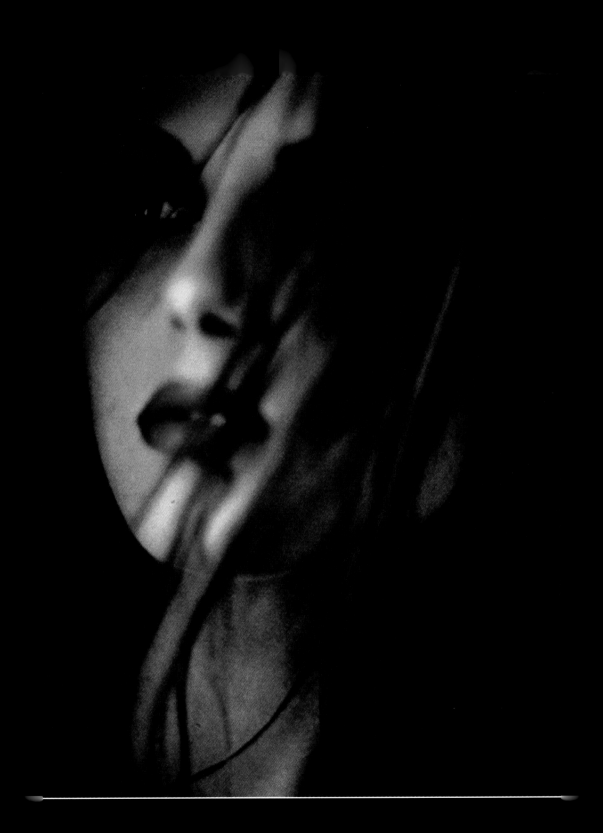

Photographer: **Frank P. Wartenberg**

Use: **Portfolio**

Hair and make-up: **Susan Swoboda**

Camera: **6x7cm**

Lens: **185mm**

Film: **Polaroid 691**

Exposure: **Not recorded; double exposure**

Lighting: **Electronic flash: 5 heads**

Props and set: **White background**

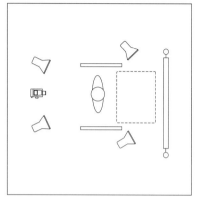

Plan View

► *Reproduction from Polaroid originals is fully feasible; this is reproduced from just part of the pack film area*

► *Exposing separately for the foreground and background gives the photographer new opportunities for control*

► *Do not always believe the instructions on film boxes which say, "Unsuitable for general photography"*

I 9 6 0 S   H A I R

▼

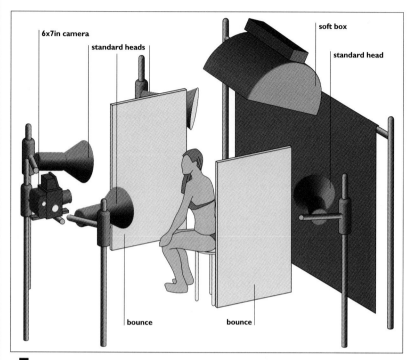

THIS IS CLASSIC "HIGH-KEY" LIGHTING. THE BACKGROUND IS STRONGLY LIT TO GET A PURE WHITE, WHILE THE MODEL'S FACE IS LIT WITH TWO STANDARD HEADS, WITH TWO SILVER BOUNCES TO EVEN OUT THE LIGHT STILL FURTHER.

An additional hair light – unusually, a soft box rather than a highly directional light – completes the lighting plot. There were two exposures: one for the model (with the background lights off), and another for the background (no light on the model).

The whole is recorded on Polaroid Type 691, an 85×105mm (3 1/2×4 1/4in) transparency pack film designed for overhead projector use. As with so many specialised Polaroid products, this is capable of delivering interesting results when used in ways other than those envisaged by the manufacturer.

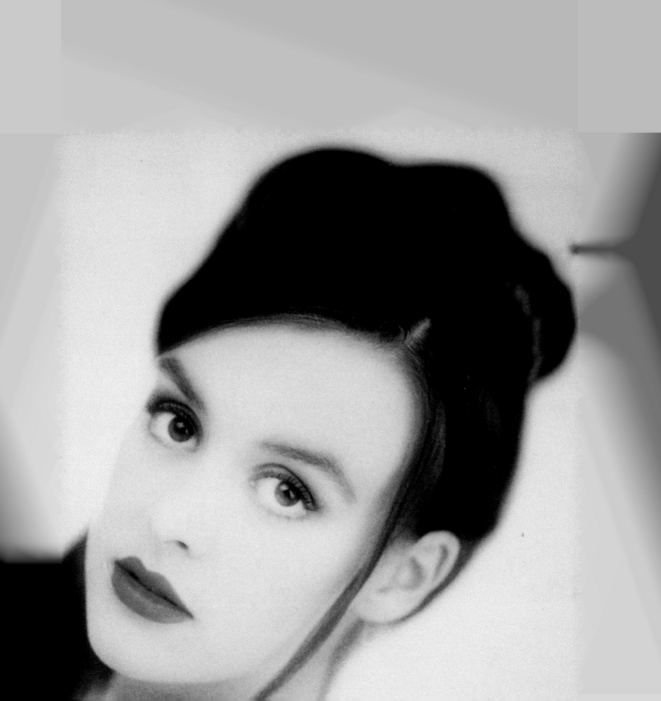

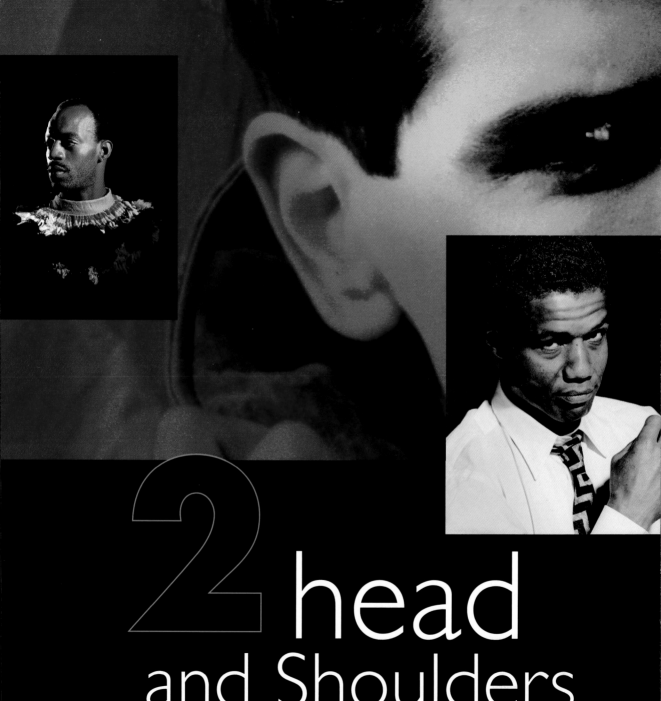

2 head
and Shoulders

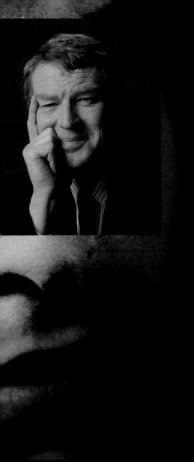

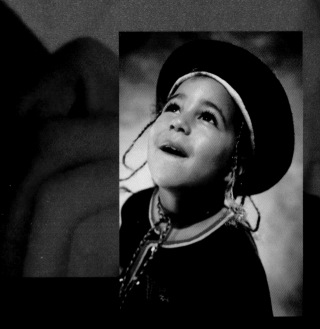

The distinction between a large head portrait and a head-and-shoulders can be blurred, but two useful generalizations may be made. One is that in a head-and-shoulders portrait, the clothing (or lack of it) worn by the subject conveys a good deal of additional information. The second is that body language can also play an important rôle: in particular, the angle of the shoulders and the position of the hands (which are often included).

Another thing which is often more important in the head-and-shoulders portrait than in the large head is the background. In a large head portrait, the background is usually plain, often without any texture whatsoever. In a head-and-shoulders, while a plain neutral background may often be appropriate, there are also times when there is a large enough area of background to require some texture or variation in lighting to stop it drawing attention to itself by its very blandness. The background is normally chosen to harmonize with the overall colour of the portrait, though dramatic effects can be achieved by using contrasting colours.

A classic trick is to shape the background lighting to the subject. This can be done to create a sort of "hot spot" surrounding him or her, or in order to create a graded ground; some backgrounds are actually painted in this way, with a lighter "hot spot" and a darker part.

Photographer: **Lewis Lang**

Use: **Exhibition/print sales**

Model: **Thomas Pelosi**

Camera: **35mm**

Lens: **85mm**

Film: **Black and white**

Exposure: **Two exposures – see text**

Lighting: **Electronic flash. First exposure: 2 standard heads, 1 soft box. Second exposure: 1 standard head, 1 soft box**

Props and set: **Brown "paper-bag" type background to bring out texture and faceted appearance**

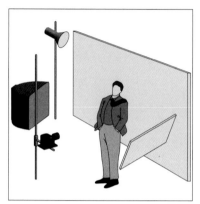

First Exposure

In a composite shot like this, it is generally easier to achieve the result in the darkroom (where dodging, burning and variable magnifications may readily be employed) rather than with a multiple exposure in a large-format camera

▶ *The photographer's role in this sort of shot is akin to that of a movie director: he and he alone has the vision of the final product in his head*

▼

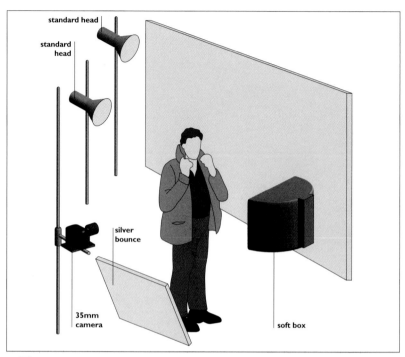

"THIS IS A COMPOSITE OF TWO BLACK AND WHITE SHOTS, PRINTED ON COLOUR (TYPE C) PAPER. THE DODGING AND BURNING NECESSARY TO MAKE THE LARGE FACE YELLOW AND TO DROP IN THE SMALLER IMAGE (TIE OVER SHOULDER) HAS ALMOST OBLITERATED THE EFFECTS OF THE ORIGINAL LIGHTING" (LEWIS LANG).

Even so, the lighting had to be consistent. The key light in the first (large-head) exposure comes from camera left. Two standard heads, one some 2m (6½ft) high and the other about 1.5m (5ft) highlight the left of the face. A medium-size soft box fills the other side of the face, and a silver bounce lightens the leather jacket.

The second exposure is lit only from camera left, with a high (2m/6½ft) standard head and a medium-sized soft box at the same height; a silver reflector to camera right provides the only fill. Neither exposure was recorded.

Photographer's comment:

The real lighting (and colour) emphasis in this composite shot has actually taken place in the enlarger! Copying the composite print onto 4x5in 'chrome and then printing that copy chrome onto Fuji Type R paper has popped both colour and contrast.

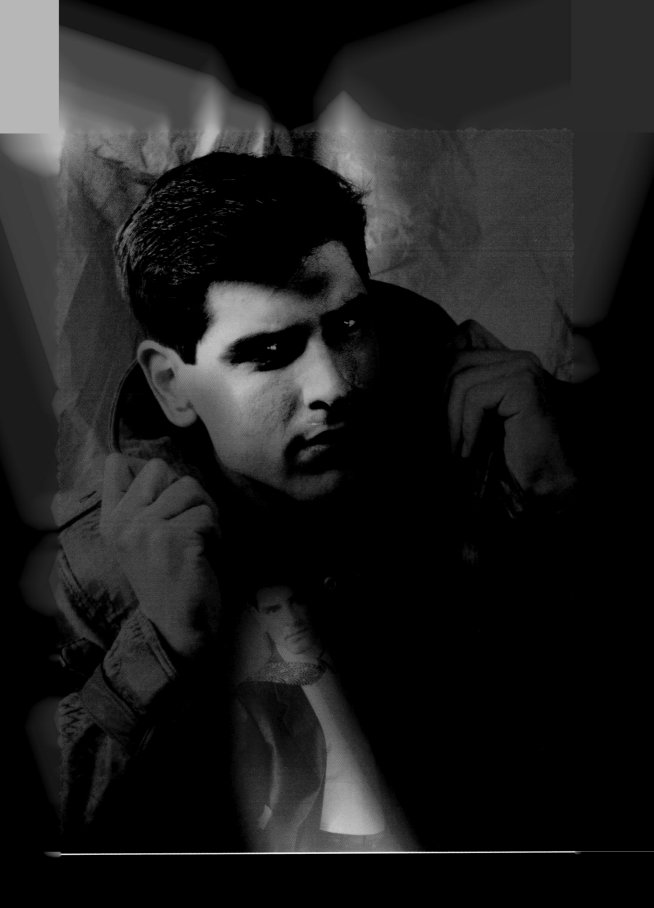

Photographer: **Harry Lomax**

Client: **Cathy**

Use: **Portfolio**

Model: **Cathy**

Camera: **4x5in**

Lens: **210mm with HiTech soft diffuser**

Film: **Fuji RDP ISO 100**

Exposure: **f/16**

Lighting: **Electronic flash: 2 heads**

Props and set: **Towel, white background**

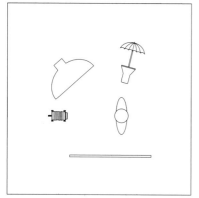

Plan View

► *On a slow day in the studio, any photographer would be well advised to try a few high-key shots (using anyone available as a model, or even a plaster mannequin) if he or she has not already mastered this technique*

► *With a seated model, it may sometimes be possible to give a double exposure: one for the background (with the model in place but unlit) and another for the model and the background together*

C A T H Y

▼

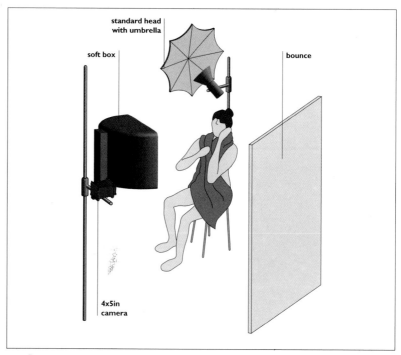

standard head
with umbrella

soft box

bounce

4x5in
camera

Iт тakes a brave man — or an experienced one — deliberately to overexpose 4x5in film in complete confidence that overexposure will deliver the effect that is wanted. But there is no such thing as correct exposure: there is only pleasing exposure.

The light, soft image has many associations. Sunlight; health; cleanliness; a sauna; exercise …. The key light is a shot-through Softstar immediately to camera right, about 60cm (2ft) above the model's eye-line and 2.5m (8ft) distant. The supplementary light is an umbrella, some 3m (10ft) away and set two stops brighter than the key. This gives the bright highlights off the hair, the glowing white of the edge of the towel, and the bright white of the background, which nevertheless is slightly darker than the towel.

White-on-white shots are always difficult to carry off, and frequently the brighter white is the foreground rather than the seemingly brilliant background. This is one of the many ways that photography differs from drawing; or at least, from drawing executed by any but the most skilled artist.

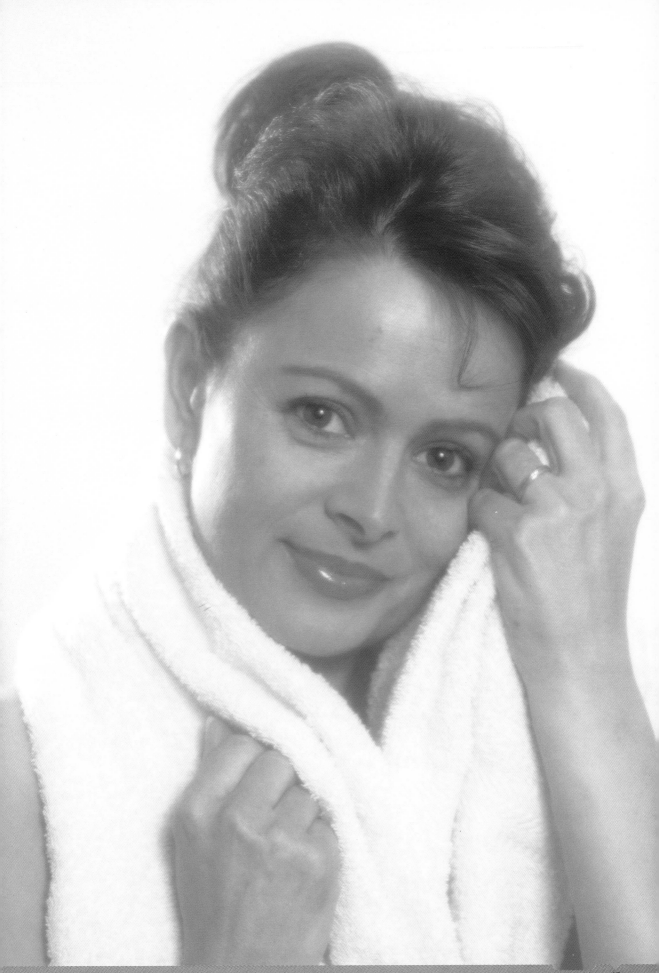

Photographer: **Roger Hicks**

Client: **Blandford Press**

Use: **Editorial**

Subject: **Dennis Richards**

Assistant: **Frank Drake**

Camera: **6x7cm**

Lens: **150mm soft focus**

Film: **Fuji RTP ISO 64**

Exposure: **Aperture f/6.3; time not recorded**

Lighting: **Tungsten: 5K focusing spot + 2K flood**

Props and set: **Black background paper**

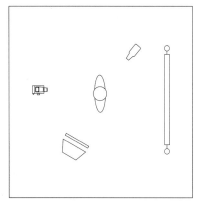

Plan View

D E N N I S   R I C H A R D S

▼

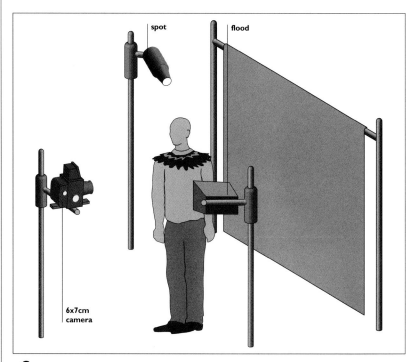

CHOICE OF FORMAT HAS CONSIDERABLE INFLUENCE ON WHAT YOU CAN GET AWAY WITH. WITH A TRUE SOFT-FOCUS LENS, 6X7CM IS AS SMALL AS IT IS SAFE TO GO; AND THE HIGHLIGHTS IN THIS SHOT HOVER ON THE EDGE OF OVEREXPOSURE.

With 35mm the highlights would be "blown" and the soft-focus would be excessive; with 4x5in or (better still) 8x10in there would be more opportunity to "see into the shadows" in the lower part of the picture. But the hair is adequately differentiated from the background, though the underside of the chin is almost lost.

The key is a 5K spot to camera left, back lighting the right cheek (to the point of overexposure) and delineating the nose clearly; but a 2K flood, diffused with a fibreglass scrim, gives the left cheek a more normal exposure. Plenty of room between the subject and the background allows the picture to come out of pure, shadowless black.

► *Surprisingly powerful tungsten lights are needed for convenient exposure times on slow colour films*

► *The eyes have a distant look: the effect would be quite different if they were turned more towards the camera*

Photographer's comment:

The deliberate overexposure of the right side of the face is meant to re-create the bright, clear light of Africa. The picture was used in my book Advanced Portrait Photography.

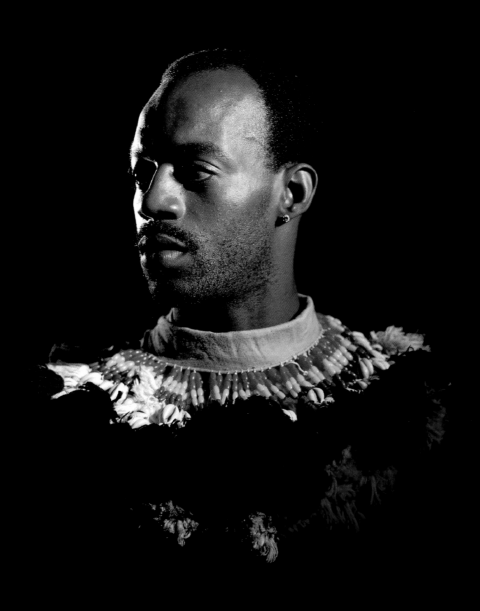

Photographer: **Massimo Robecchi**

Client: **Muster & Dikson**

Use: **Poster**

Model: **Ann**

Assistant and stylist: **Teresa La Grotteria**

Make up and hair: **Gianluca Rolandi**

Camera: **35mm**

Lens: **135mm**

Film: **Polaroid Polapan 35mm**

Exposure: **1/8 second at f/8**

Lighting: **Flash + tungsten**

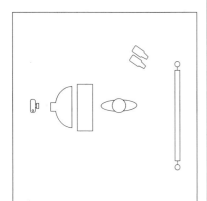

Plan View

B L A C K   A N D   W H I T E
P O R T R A I T

▼

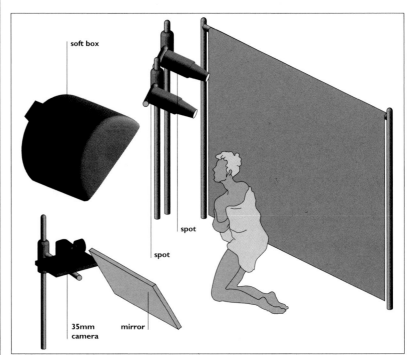

$\mathbf{T}$HE LUMINESCENT MONOCHROME OF THIS PICTURE SEEMS TO OWE A DEBT TO THE GREAT DAYS OF HOLLYWOOD IN THE 1940S, WHILE THE GIRL'S LOOKS ECHO THE CLASSICAL GLAMOUR OF THE 1970S; YET THERE IS SOMETHING TOTALLY MODERN IN THE OVERALL EFFECT.

The choice of Polaroid's remarkable Polapan material helps to create this mood of spanning the decades, but a great deal also depends on lighting: the tonality is very subtle indeed, with a short tonal range. And yet the lighting is extremely simple. A single, large soft box, about 1x2m (3x6½ft), directly overhead defines the tonality and creates the highlights on the model's shoulders, while fill comes from a mirror placed below. Two tungsten spots create the streaks on the wall behind the model; the long exposure was necessary to balance the tungsten and flash exposures.

► With a large enough key, a mirror can be used as a fill to create a very even light without "hot spots"

► Polapan gives wonderful effects but the emulsion is very fragile: it is wise to send out duplicates rather than originals

Photographer's comment:

The model moved slightly during the exposure, as you can see from the shadow effect in the hair and at the right shoulder.

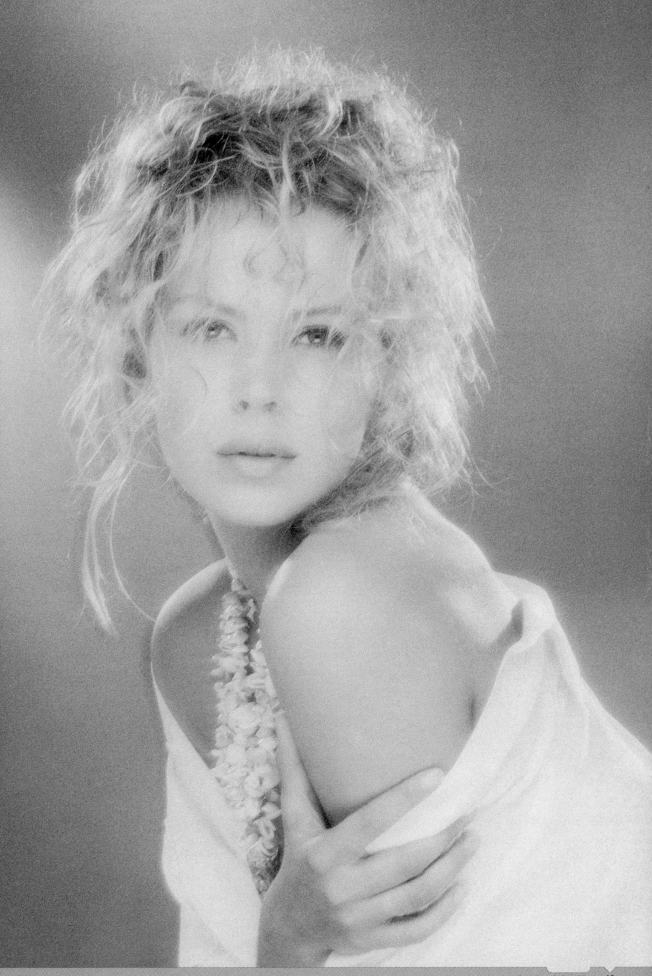

Photographer: **Colin Glanfield**

Use: **Publicity/portfolio**

Subject: **Rt. Hon. Paddy Ashdown, M.P.**

Camera: **8x10in**

Lens: **360mm (14in)**

Film: **Kodak Ektachrome Type 6118 ISO 64**

Exposure: **f/11**

Lighting: **Electronic flash: 2 heads**

Props and set: **Hand-painted background**

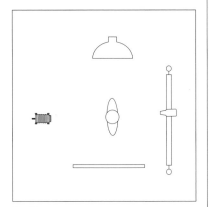

Plan View

► *Even elderly 8x10in cameras and lenses can give wonderful character portraits*

► *There is no need for very powerful lights, as working apertures are normally around f/11 or larger*

► *Very large formats are best suited to formal or semi-formal portraits*

PADDY ASHDOWN

▼

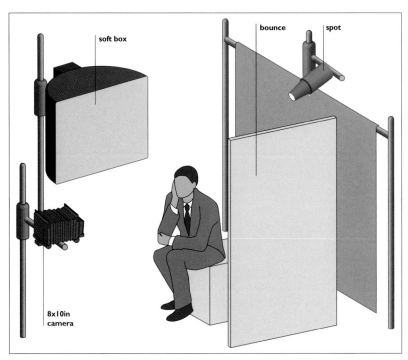

"I WANTED THIS AS A PORTFOLIO SHOT; I WAS CONSIDERING A BOOK ON EMINENT FIGURES OF PADDY'S (AND MY) GENERATION — PEOPLE OVER ABOUT 50. SINCE THEN, HE HAS REQUESTED SEVERAL HUNDRED COPIES OF THIS PICTURE."

Portraiture with 8x10in cameras is rare nowadays, but it gives a quality which is not readily obtainable with smaller formats. There is no need for a great deal of power in the lighting, as 8x10 portraiture is traditionally carried out at, or close to, full aperture.

The key light was a 1000 joule head in a medium-sized soft box: a 90x120cm (3x4ft) "Super Fish Frier", set to camera left, with modest fill from a 120x240cm (4x8ft) white bounce to camera right. Another 1000 joule head, heavily snooted and knocked back with scrims, looked down from above the hand-painted background. It served principally as a hair light, though not in the usual back light sense.

Photographer's comment:

I shot this with a 14in f/6.3 uncoated Tessar, which is neither a conventional soft focus lens nor as bitingly sharp (at least at full aperture) as a modern high-quality objective.

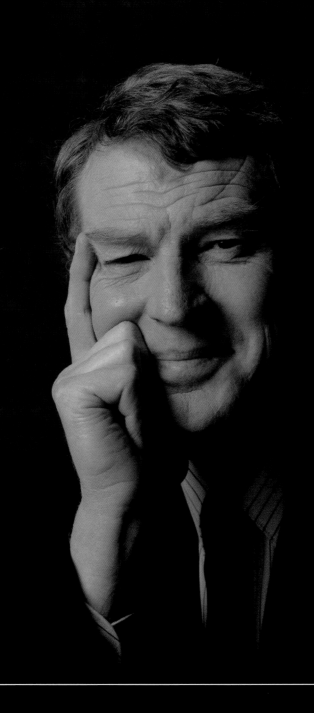

Photographer: **Alan Sheldon**

Client: **Gulliver (Japanese travel magazine)**

Use: **Editorial**

Camera: **645**

Lens: **150mm**

Film: **Fujichrome RDP ISO 100**

Exposure: **1/125 second at f/8**

Lighting: **Daylight**

Props and set: **Location**

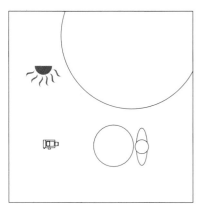

Plan View

R I C H A R D   B R A N S O N

▼

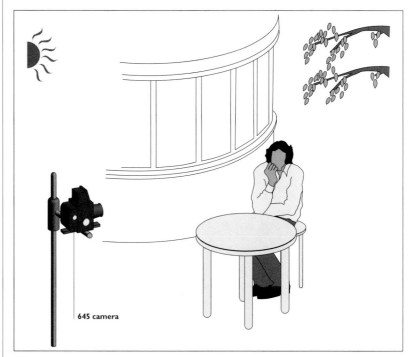

645 camera

THIS IS AN ABSOLUTELY STRAIGHT DAYLIGHT SHOT, WITH NO LIGHT MODIFIERS, NO FILL FLASH, NOTHING: JUST A VERY CAREFUL CHOICE OF LOCATION, AND EXTREMELY PRECISE EXPOSURE. CHOOSING FUJI RDP, WITH ITS INHERENTLY LONG TONAL RANGE, WAS CRUCIAL: VELVIA WOULD NOT HAVE WORKED.

Unusually, the photographer says that he exposed for the shadows and let the highlights take care of themselves: a common enough approach in monochrome, but rather less usual in colour. The result is that much of the shirt hovers on the edge of over-exposure, and the window frame behind Richard Branson is very bright indeed;

but it all works. What is more, this is true sunlight, not overcast light, which is easier to handle from a contrast point of view but is very blue and dull from a pictorial viewpoint. The directionality and warmth of the light is very important, though reflected light from a variety of sources does create a good deal of natural fill.

► *Fair skin, fair hair and a light shirt allow very slight (about 1/3 stop) under-exposure without making for an unnaturally dark complexion*

► *The eyes are slightly narrowed against the sun, but the impression is of intelligence and calculation rather than squinting*

Photographer's comment:

Every shot from this session features the hand covering the mouth. Why? He had a chapped lip, and we didn't want it to show.

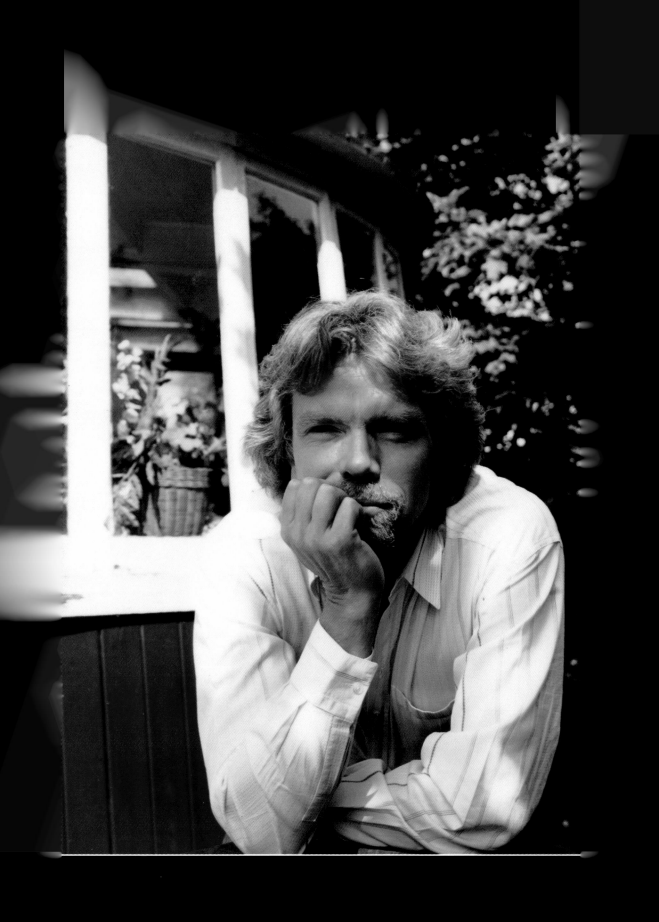

Photographer: **Alan Sheldon**

Client: **20th Century Fox**

Use: **Press/publicity**

Camera: **645**

Lens: **80mm**

Film: **Kodak Tri-X Pan at ISO 320**

Exposure: **1/60 second at f/11**

Lighting: **Electronic flash: 3 heads**

Props and set: **White background paper**

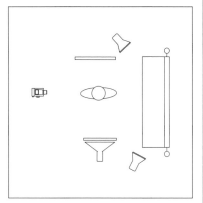

Plan View

► *Even in portraiture, depth of field is sometimes important: the hands would not "work" if they were not sharp*

► *Even the smallest roll-film format, 645, can deliver exquisite texture and detail*

► *Broad areas of extreme tone (the jacket, the background) are well balanced by areas of detail and texture (the face, the hand, the tie)*

M E L   B R O O K S

▼

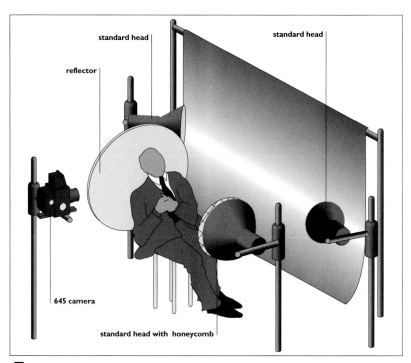

standard head

standard head

reflector

645 camera

standard head with honeycomb

THE LIGHTING OF THIS PORTRAIT IS SUBSTANTIALLY IDENTICAL TO THAT OF THE LARGE HEAD PORTRAIT ON PAGE 33, BUT IT ILLUSTRATES HOW MUCH DIFFERENCE CAN BE MADE BY POSE AND BY SWITCHING FROM COLOUR TO MONOCHROME.

A light with a large honeycombed reflector, about 30cm (12in) square, to camera right, almost at right angles to the line of sight but slightly in front of the subject's eyes, provides the key. Kodak Tri-X Pan, rated at its full speed, is fairly contrasty and very dramatic. There is a Lastolite reflector just out of shot, to camera left, to provide fill; and some more fill comes from reflections from the brightly lit background, which is illuminated by two standard heads. All three lights (key and two background) are 500 joule units. Everything – lights and background included – was brought to the location for the portrait.

Photographer's comment:

This was one of my earliest portraits. Looking at it now, the hands seem rather too big – they would have been better with a 150mm – but they still serve as a useful counterbalance to the face.

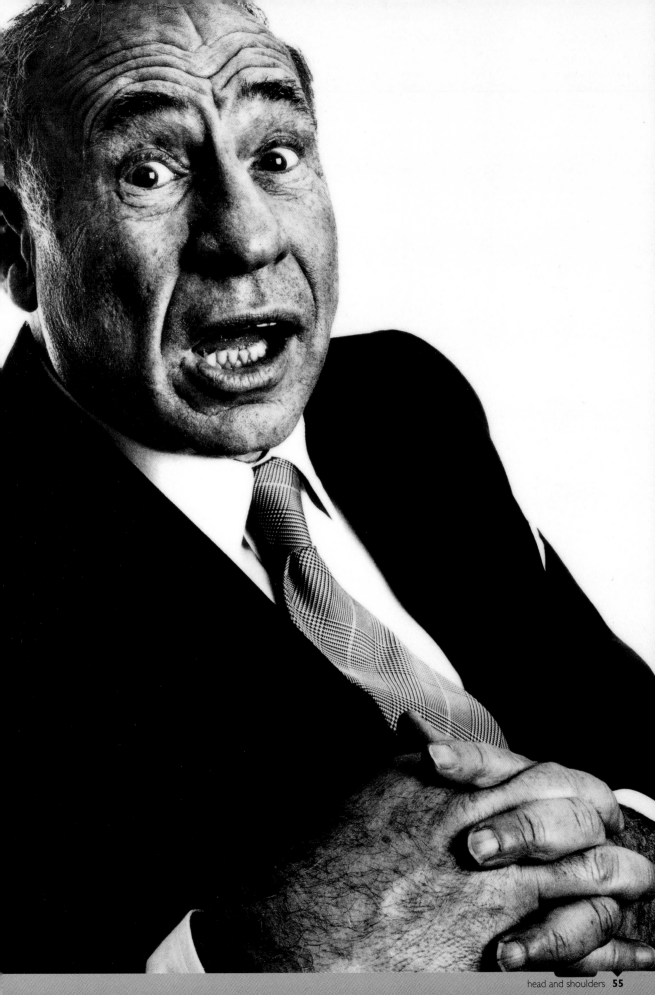

Photographer: **Alan Sheldon**

Client: **Slags (hatters)**

Use: **Editorial**

Assistant: **Dave Hindley**

Camera: **645**

Lens: **150mm with short extension tube**

Film: **Fujichrome RDP ISO 100**

Exposure: **1/30 second at f/11**

Lighting: **Tungsten**

Props and set: **Painted backdrop**

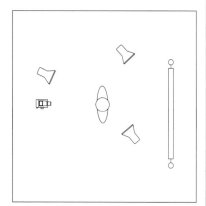

Plan View

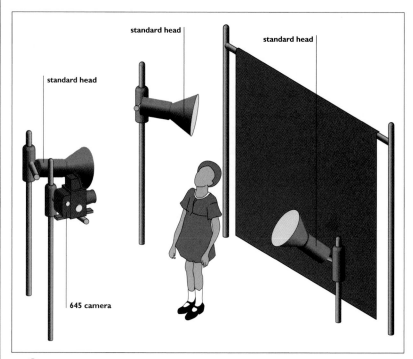

SOME DAYLIGHT-BALANCED FILMS REACT MUCH BETTER TO TUNGSTEN LIGHTING THAN OTHERS, AND FUJI FILMS (WHICH ARE WARM TO BEGIN WITH) RESPOND SURPRISINGLY WELL. THIS WAS LIT ONLY WITH TUNGSTEN LIGHTING, USING THREE HEADS: A KEY LIGHT, A BACK LIGHT, AND A BACKGROUND LIGHT.

The key light is a standard head to camera left, but at a fairly acute angle to the line of sight of the camera and rather above the subject's eye-line. Going to the edge of overexposure means very bright highlights but it helps to hold the colours and textures in the hat and clothes and is no problem in the light of the model's dark complexion; it also "works" well when shooting daylight film under tungsten lights.

A second light behind the model and very slightly to camera right serves to differentiate the hat from the background – look at the very edge – and a third light is shaped to give a "hot spot" on the painted backdrop.

► *Err on the side of overexposure when shooting daylight film under tungsten lights*

► *Hair lights and similar back lights should be used with caution as they are easily overdone*

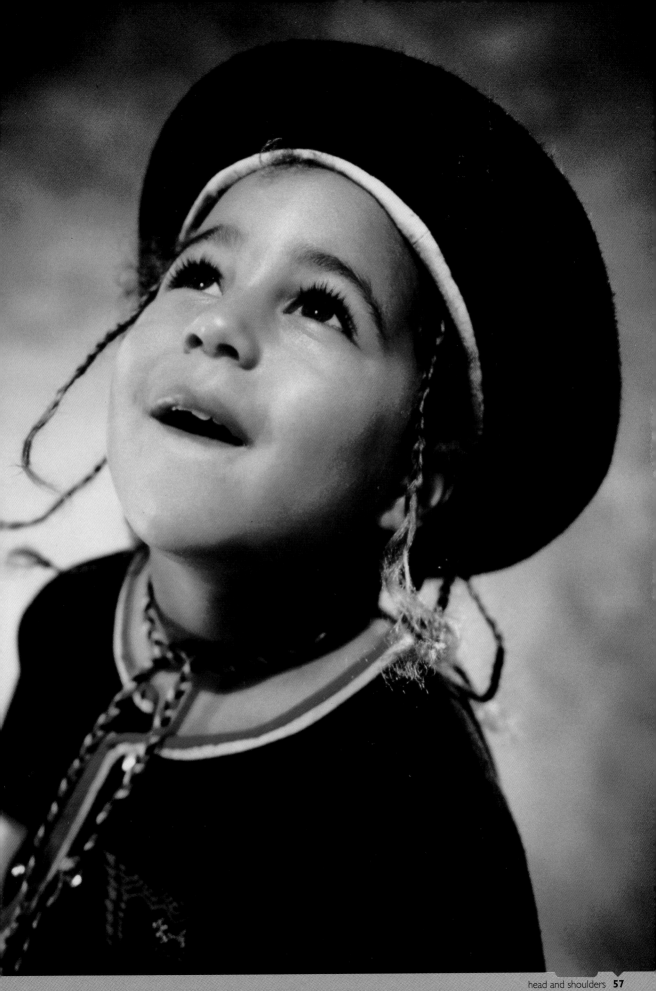

Photographer: **Alan Sheldon**

Client: **ES Magazine**

Use: **Editorial**

Assistant: **Quintin Wright**

Camera: **6x6cm**

Lens: **150mm**

Film: **Kodak Tri-X rated at EI 200**

Exposure: **1/60 second at f/8**

Lighting: **Electronic flash: 3 heads**

Props and set: **Location studio (see text)**

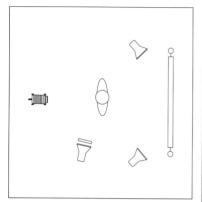

Plan View

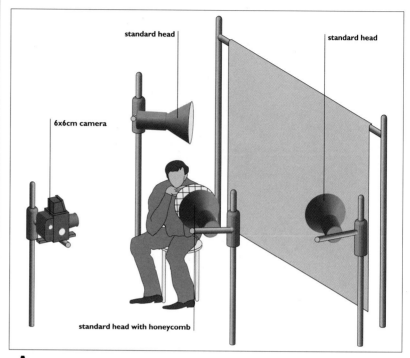

ALTHOUGH HE WORKS IN MANY OTHER AREAS AS WELL, ALAN SHELDON IS PARTICULARLY WELL KNOWN FOR HIS "PORTABLE STUDIO" TECHNIQUE: HE CARRIES WITH HIM NOT JUST HIS LIGHTING BUT ALSO HIS BACKGROUNDS AND EVEN (IF NECESSARY) A GENERATOR.

This was shot in the rehearsal room at a theatre, in between all the other things that go on at a rehearsal: the actual photographic session lasted no more than 15 to 20 minutes. The print is selenium toned. The key light is a 500 joule light with a standard reflector and a medium honeycomb, to camera right at about 45° to the line of sight; the shadows clearly show the angle. The only other light is on the background, where two standard heads burn the white paper out to a clear, bright maximum white.

► *Portable background stands and a roll of seamless paper can transform location portraits*

► *There is a difference between a pure white background and an overlit or apparently luminous background*

► *This is a rare example of a genuinely square composition in the square format*

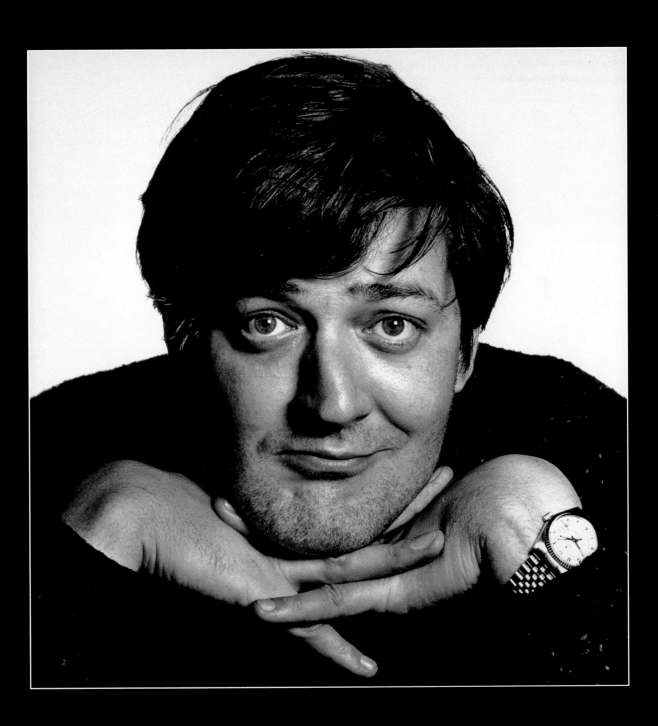

Photographer: **Johnny Boylan**

Client: **Royal Shakespeare Company**

Use: **Poster for** *Faust*

Assistant: **Belinda Pickering**

Camera: **6x7cm**

Lens: **180mm**

Film: **Agfa APX 100**

Exposure: **f/11**

Lighting: **Electronic flash: one head**

Props and set: **Painted grey background**

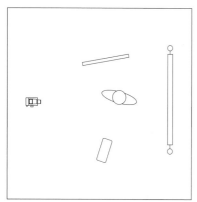

Plan View

► *Monochrome films can deliver superb skin texture*

► *Different skins differ not only in tone but also in the way that they handle highlights: some are shinier than others*

► *Adaptation of big old tungsten lights to flash can create some interesting light sources*

M E P H I S T O P H E L E S

▼

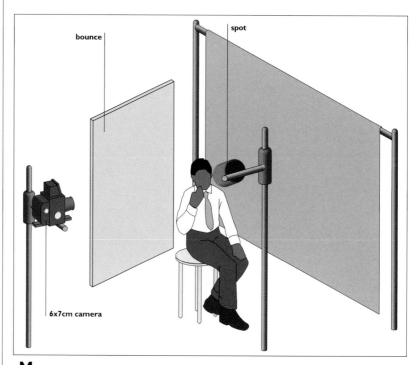

MEPHISTOPHELES COMES IN MANY GUISES; HERE HE IS SMOOTH, URBANE, READY TO STRIKE A DEAL, ALWAYS WILLING TO COMPROMISE — UNTIL HE HAS YOUR SOUL, WHEN SUDDENLY HIS TRUE NATURE IS REVEALED. QUITE LIKE THE AVERAGE CLIENT, REALLY.

Lighting dark skin presents different challenges from lighting light skin because highlights tend to be brighter and shadows darker.

The key and only light is high and from camera right; the shadows show clearly where it is coming from. The light itself is unusual: an old 2K focusing spot with the hot light source replaced by a flash head. A number of photographers have made similar conversions of big old hot lights because they give a unique quality of light: a relatively large source, yet highly directional.

The lighting set-up is completed with a white bounce for a fill to camera left, described by the photographer as a "half poly board"; in other words, a 120x120cm (4x4ft) white polystyrene reflector, half of a full 4x8ft sheet.

Photographer's comment:

I like Agfa APX because it delivers contrast which is both gentle and clear: not harsh, but not flat either.

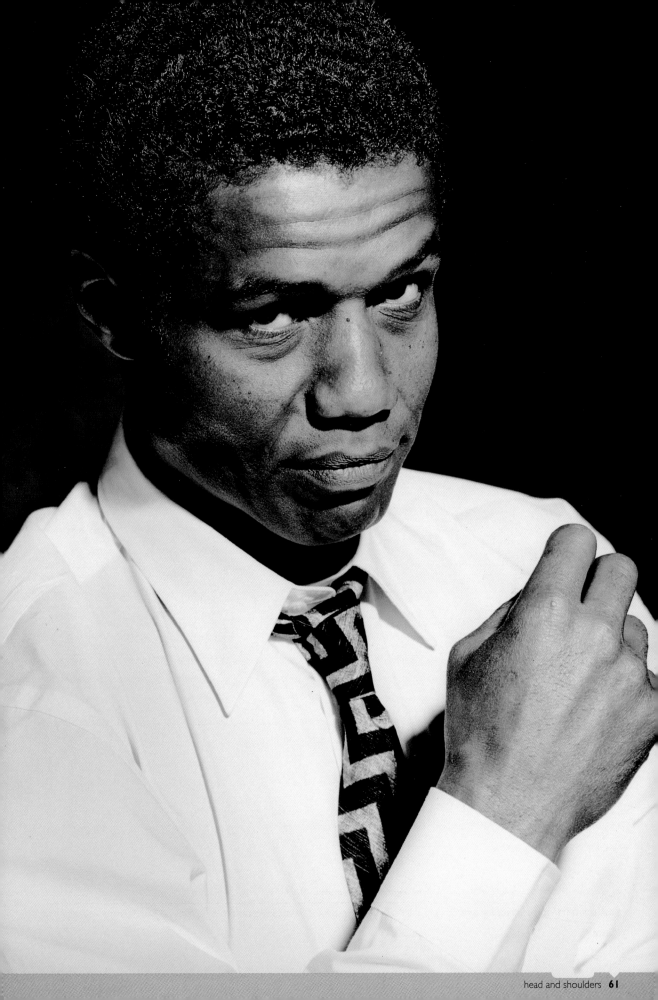

Photographer: **Struan**

Client: ***Art Director's Index***

Use: **Book cover**

Model: **Trish**

Make-up: **Kelly Jackson**

Hair: **Shirley Lang**

Camera: **6x6cm**

Lens: **150mm**

Film: **Kodak Tri-X Pan**

Exposure: **f/11**

Lighting: **Electronic flash: one projection (optical) spot, one standard head with honeycomb**

Props and set: **Gobo for projection spot; "earring"; white background**

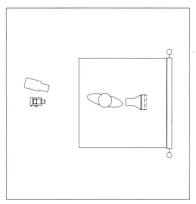

Plan View

▼

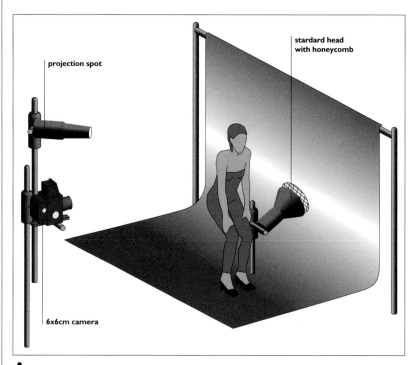

AS WITH MANY OF STRUAN'S PHOTOGRAPHS, THIS IS A WORK OF DECEPTIVE SIMPLICITY. THERE ARE ONLY TWO LIGHTS, ONE ON THE GIRL AND ONE ON THE BACKGROUND; BUT THE ATTENTION TO DETAIL IS WONDERFUL.

The key light is, in the photographer's own words, "an optical spot beside my left ear, with about 2400 Watt-seconds running through it – those things eat a lot of light." The interior mask or gobo creates the V-shape of light. The "earring" was in fact a piece of silver card cut to echo the shape of the V of light, and two hair pieces were added to create the curling shapes that contrast with the angular patch of light.

The background is lit with a single 400 Joule standard head, honeycombed for directionality, pointing back to illuminate the white background and grading it from bottom to top.

► *Projection spots are expensive – but they can be rented*

► *The simpler the shot, the more attention you have to pay to detail*

Photographer's comment:

I often use just one light, and because I'm left handed I like it where I can move it easily with my left hand. The eyes were hand-painted green.

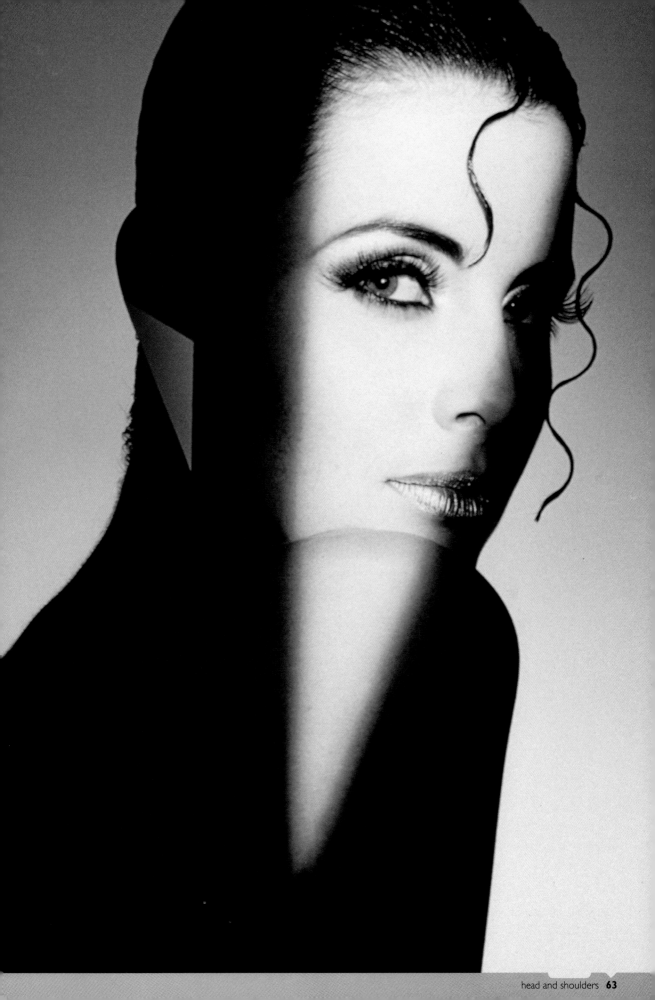

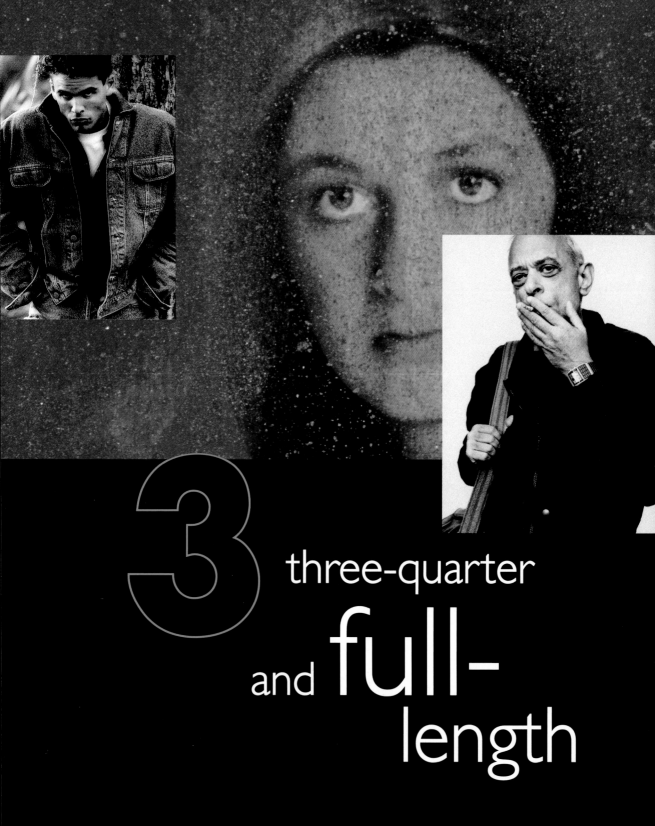

3

three-quarter
and full-
length

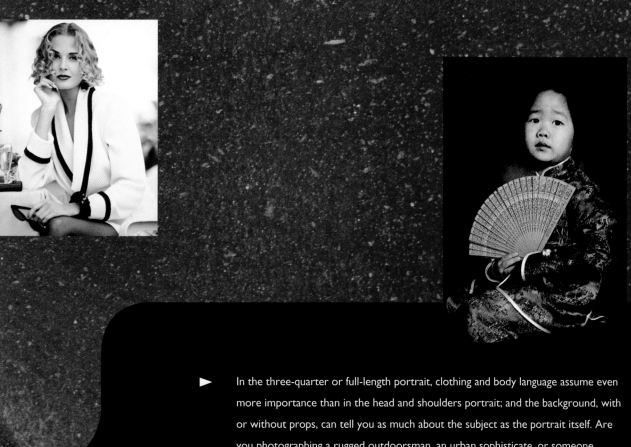

► In the three-quarter or full-length portrait, clothing and body language assume even more importance than in the head and shoulders portrait; and the background, with or without props, can tell you as much about the subject as the portrait itself. Are you photographing a rugged outdoorsman, an urban sophisticate, or someone relaxing in casual surroundings?

In the formal studio portrait, backgrounds are often conventionalized. Our ancestors habitually used elaborate representational backgrounds, as if (for example) the sitter were on the balcony of a country house. These are still available from specialised suppliers, but they are more rarely used today. Now, overwhelmingly the most commonly encountered conventional background is a painted canvas backdrop with an irregular but still basically repetitive pattern.

In the nature of things, lighting ratios on the subject proper are often fairly tight, typically at a stop or less, so as to reveal the clothing and other props. This does not mean that the lighting is flat and frontal. Again and again in portraiture, the truth is demonstrated that a strongly directional key light will always give good modelling, right up to the point where it is completely swamped by a soft fill.

It is also worth noting that while three-quarter and full-length portraits are often of their time, it is possible to create something very different by deliberately going back to the ultra-formalism and Sunday Best clothes of our forebears, or to break all the rules and create something which owes more to Francis Bacon than to Rembrandt.

Photographer: **Clive Stewart**

Use: **Self promotion**

Camera: **6x7cm**

Lens: **180mm plus vignette and soft focus screen**

Film: **Ilford FP4**

Exposure: **f/8**

Lighting: **Electronic flash: 3 heads**

Props and set: **Painted canvas backdrop**

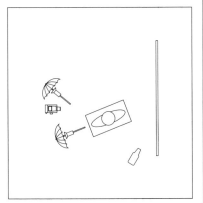

Plan View

► *Different umbrellas (silver and white) give different qualities of light*

► *Choosing monochrome films for portraiture is an intensely personal business, but many photographers reckon that they get better results with "old-technology" films like Ilford FP4 than with "new-technology" films like Ilford Delta 100*

C H I N E S E   G I R L

▼

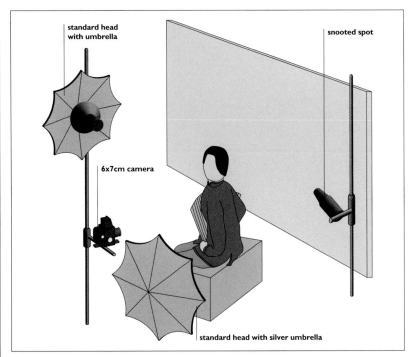

standard head with umbrella

snooted spot

6x7cm camera

standard head with silver umbrella

IF EVER PROOF WERE NEEDED OF THE FACT THAT, TODAY, 6X7CM CAN REPLACE 4X5IN EVEN FOR THE MOST TRADITIONAL PORTRAITS, THIS IS IT — THOUGH SOFT, DIRECTIONAL LIGHTING, VERY SKILLFULLY USED, STILL FURTHER CALLS TO MIND THE DAYLIGHT STUDIOS OF OUR ANCESTORS.

The key light is a silver umbrella to camera right, 1.5m (5ft) above the ground, with fill provided by another umbrella directly above the camera, which itself is about 1m (40in) off the ground. The technique of using a silver umbrella for extra directionality and reflectivity, and a white umbrella for a softer fill, is well worth remembering. As usual with successful portraits, there is plenty of room between the model and the background: about 2m (6½ft). This prevents spill from the main lights illuminating the background, which is separately lit with a snooted spot.

A home-made vignette and a very weak soft focus screen completes the set-up: soft focus screens normally work better and better as formats get larger, and with 6x7cm they are fine.

Photographer's comment:

My aim was simplicity with regard to lighting and props, thereby allowing the model's expression to dominate.

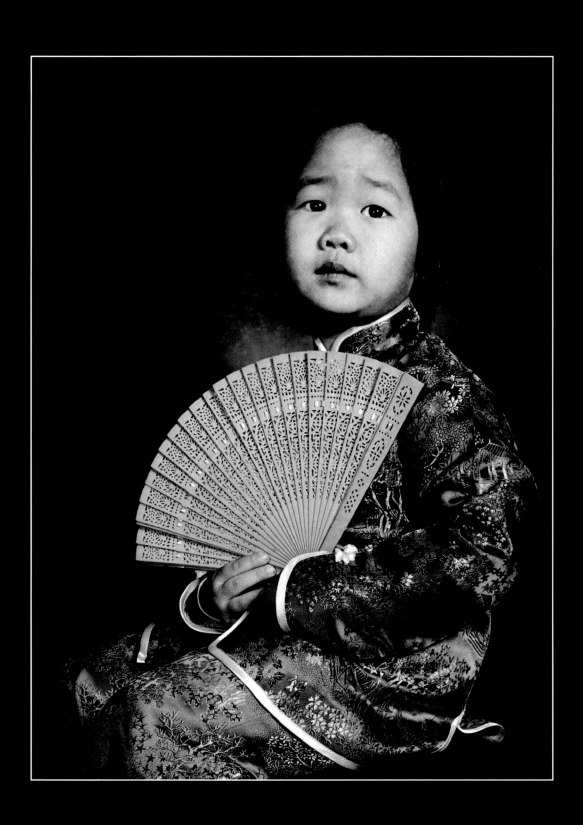

Photographer: **Kay Hurst, K Studios**

Use: **Exhibition**

Model: **Kate Maneckshaw**

Assistant: **Katy Niker**

Camera: **645**

Lens: **75mm**

Film: **Kodak T-Max 100**

Exposure: **f/11**

Lighting: **Electronic flash: 2 standard heads, 1 soft box**

Props and set: **Fabric "tent": print heavily reworked**

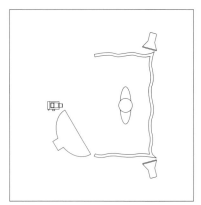

Plan View

► *"Tents" of translucent or diffusing fabric can also be very effective when employed in conjunction with more conventional high-key, soft-focus techniques*

► *The two best ways to create an impression of antiquity while retaining photographic quality are with grainy, overexposed, low-saturation images or with the sometimes vivid colours of hand tinting*

R E D   S A R I

▼

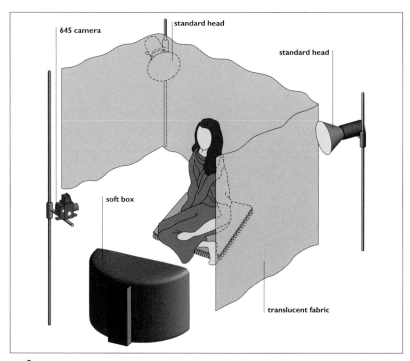

Lᴉᴋᴇ ᴍᴀɴʏ ᴏғ Kᴀʏ's ᴘɪᴄᴛᴜʀᴇs, ᴛʜɪs ɪs ʜᴇᴀᴠɪʟʏ ʀᴇᴡᴏʀᴋᴇᴅ; ʙᴜᴛ ᴛʜᴇ ʟɪɢʜᴛɪɴɢ ɪs ᴍᴏʀᴇ ᴄᴏᴍᴘʟᴇx ᴛʜᴀɴ ɪᴛ sᴇᴇᴍs. Tʜᴇ ᴋᴇʏ ʟɪɢʜᴛ ɪs sɪᴍᴘʟᴇ ᴇɴᴏᴜɢʜ – ᴀ sᴏғᴛ ʙᴏx ᴛᴏ ᴄᴀᴍᴇʀᴀ ʀɪɢʜᴛ – ʙᴜᴛ ᴛʜᴇ ʙᴀᴄᴋɢʀᴏᴜɴᴅ ɪs ɪɴᴛᴇʀᴇsᴛɪɴɢ.

The subject is sitting, enclosed on three sides in a tent of translucent fabric, which is back lit by two standard heads to bring out the texture and drape of the cloth. She is also sitting on an Indian-patterned throw.

The original black and white image was printed onto Kentmere Art Classic paper, and the vivid colour of the sari was added with photo dyes; it was actually red in the original, too. Other details were added in dye, then the whole picture was reworked with a heavy, fairly dry gouache. Finally, it was mounted on hardboard and varnished to give the cracked, antiqued appearance. Although much of the detail of both the lighting and the backgrounds is obliterated by the after-work, enough of it remains to create the impression of a carefully-made picture which has weathered many years.

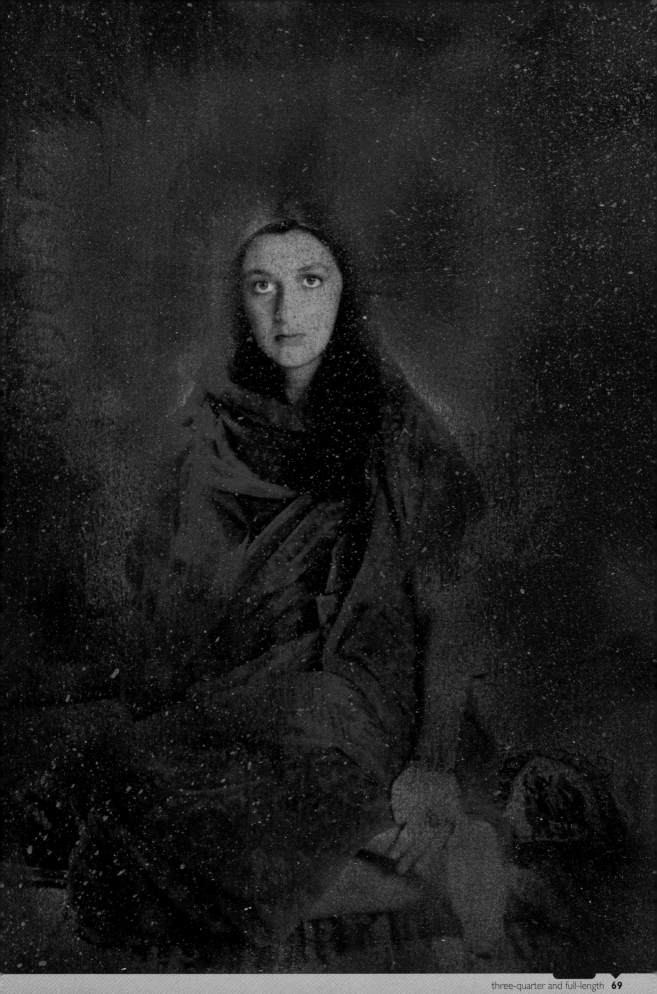

Photographer: **Massimo Robecchi**

Client: **Studio Magazine**

Use: **Editorial**

Model: **Susan**

Assistant and stylist: **Teresa La Grotteria**

Art director: **Olga Stavel**

Make-up and hair: **Gianluca Rolandi**

Camera: **35mm**

Lens: **300mm**

Film: **Ilford XP2 ISO 400**

Exposure: **1/500 second at f/2.8**

Lighting: **Available light + bounce**

Props and set: **Location**

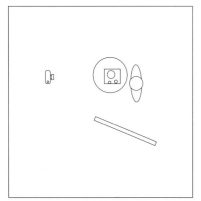

Plan View

S U S A N

▼

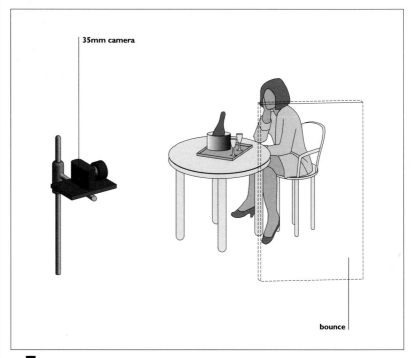

THIS PICTURE WELL ILLUSTRATES THAT AN OVERCAST DAY CAN BE VASTLY SUPERIOR TO SUNSHINE, ESPECIALLY IF YOU ARE SHOOTING IN MONOCHROME. WITH LIGHT COMING MORE OR LESS EVENLY FROM ALL DIRECTIONS, THE TONALITY CAN BE EXQUISITE.

Even so, Massimo Robecchi added a white bounce in front of the model to even out the light still further: the white drop of the table-cloth is thereby brought nearer to the tone of the clothes and the background, and the dark stockings are made to read just a little better. This is one of those cases where a collapsible reflector such as a Lastolite or a Scrim Jim can be extremely useful – and where the effect is completely different from fill-flash, touted by camera manufacturers as the answer to everything.

► *Exposure is a subjective art: arguably, everything in this picture is just a tiny bit darker than it "really" is, but this holds the tones in the white clothing*

► *A 300mm lens, used wide open at f/2.8, allows the background to be suggested rather than too clearly delineated*

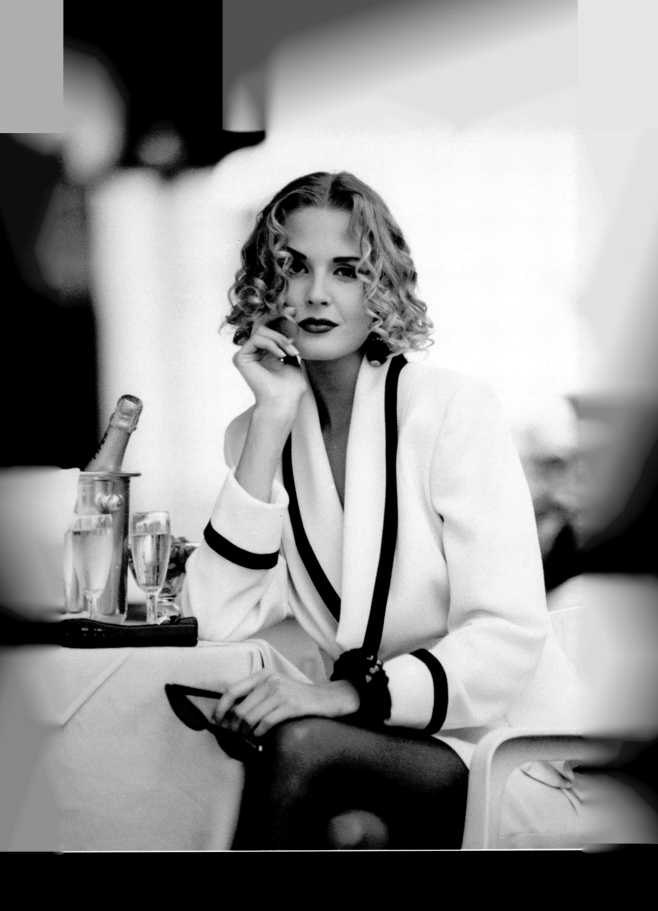

Photographer: **Alan Sheldon**

Use: **Personal research**

Model: **Passer-by on King's Road**

Assistant: **Nick Henry**

Camera: **4x5in**

Lens: **180mm**

Film: **Kodak Tri-X rated at EI 200**

Exposure: **1/60 second at f/5.6**

Lighting: **Daylight plus tungsten plus flash (see text)**

Props and set: **Built "sentry box" (see text)**

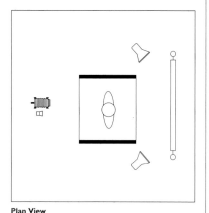

Plan View

K I N G S   R O A D   P O R T R A I T

▼

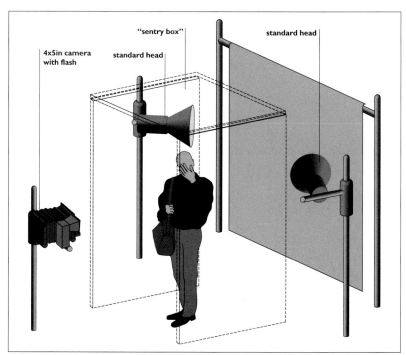

THE LEADING EXPONENT OF THIS STYLE — THE CHARACTER PORTRAIT AGAINST A FEATURELESS WHITE BACKGROUND — IS WITHOUT DOUBT AVEDON. UNASHAMEDLY FOLLOWING THE LEAD OF THE MASTER, ALAN SHELDON HAS EXPLORED THE SAME TECHNIQUES IN BOTH COLOUR AND MONOCHROME.

This was shot on the King's Road in Chelsea, London. The uprights of the "sentry box" were made of 240x120cm (8x4ft) sheets of expanded polystyrene, painted black; the roof was a half sheet, 120x120cm (4x4ft). The whole was held together with gaffer tape and meat skewers.

The box is about 1.8m (6ft) in front of a white backdrop — another 240x120cm (8x4ft) sheet — which is lit with two 800 Watt tungsten lamps powered by a generator. This gives a bright, neutral background, while the black sides and roof ensure that the only light on the subject is frontal daylight.

► A "very small" flashgun on the camera (power not recorded) gives the catch-light in the eyes

► Increased exposure and decreased development allow the film to capture a long tonal range

Photographer's comment:

After this series I went to a 3x3m (10x10ft) backdrop: I had trouble with the edges of the 240x120cm drop getting in the picture.

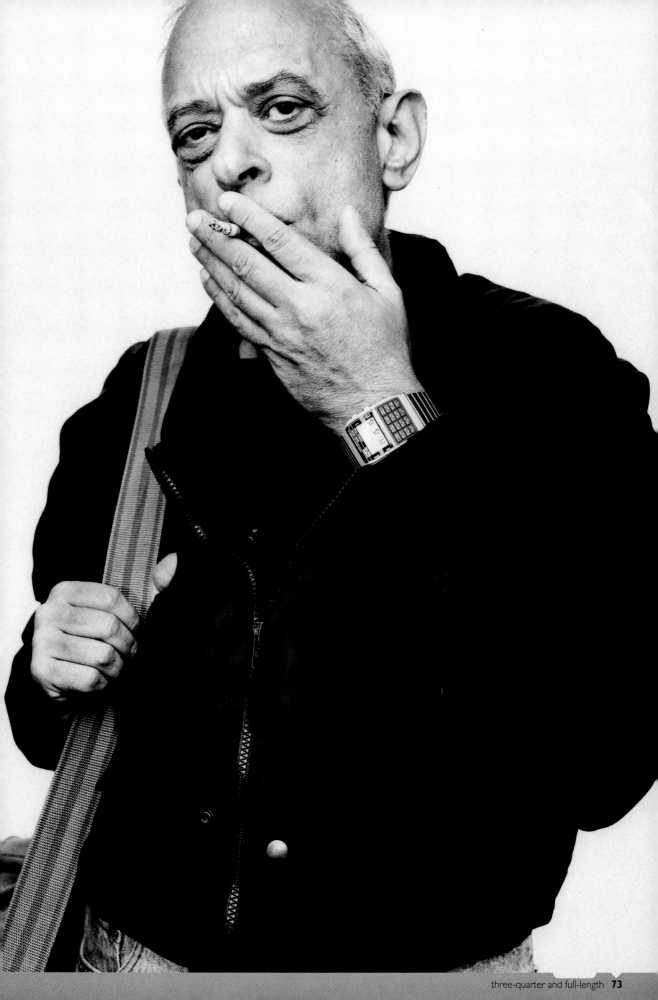

Photographer: **Johnny Boylan**

Client: **Lee Jeans**

Use: **Advertising**

Model: **Rufus (from Storm agency)**

Assistant: **Siri Hills**

Art director: **Richard Stevens**

Camera: **35mm**

Lens: **200mm**

Film: **Kodak Tri-X rated at EI 1600; toned print**

Exposure: **Not recorded; maybe 1/500 at f/11**

Lighting: **Daylight**

Props and set: **Location**

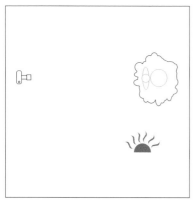

Plan View

► *"Pushed" fast films often exhibit surprisingly subtle tonality*

► *Grain can be an integral part of an image. "Old-technology" films, or Kodak TMZ P3200 pushed beyond EI 5000, give the most grain*

▼

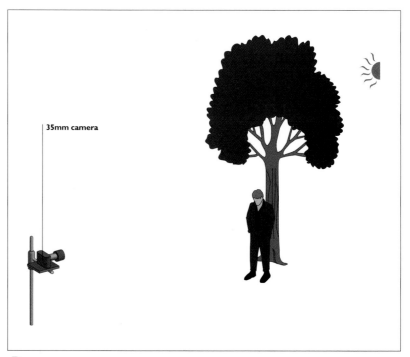

DAYLIGHT IS AN OBVIOUS CHOICE FOR THE NATURAL LOOK, AND 35MM OFTEN HAS A SENSE OF IMMEDIACY WHICH IS NOT READILY OBTAINABLE WITH LARGER FORMATS. THIS IS HOWEVER A VERY LONG WAY FROM THE CASUAL SNAPSHOT IT SEEMS TO EVOKE.

To begin with, the choice of "pushed" Tri-X adds its own note of gritty realism. Although Johnny Boylan normally uses Agfa APX in black and white, he switched to a faster, grainier, "old-technology" film and then accentuated its vintage qualities by pushing it to EI 1600. Not one person in a hundred who saw the advertisement would know how it was done, but they would recognize the James Dean/Marlon Brando 1950s style.

A 200mm lens compresses perspective for a strongly graphic appearance, and creates a shallow depth of field. Choice of focal length in fashion photography is itself fashionable – in the 1960s it was all wide-angles – but here a long lens has been used to echo the cinematic style: in the movies, close-ups like this are often made with surprisingly long lenses.

Finally, choosing the right tree, and the right side of the tree, so that the light falls right (the subject is shaded by the tree), distinguishes the skilled photographer from the snapshotter.

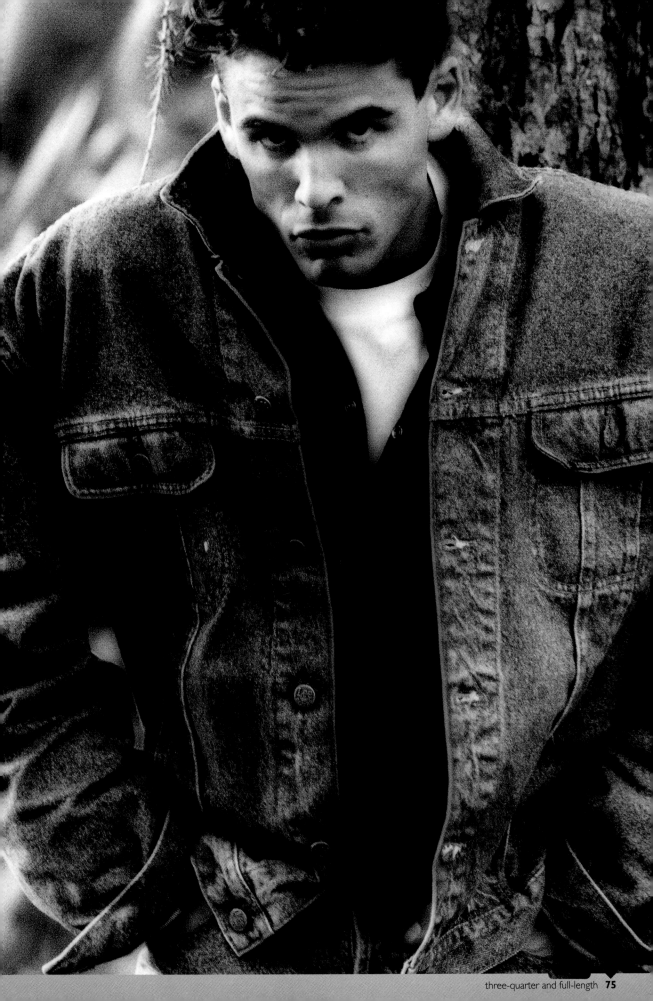

Photographer: **Maria Cristina Cassinelli**

Client: **Swissair**

Use: **Advertising**

Art director: **Carlos Gerard & Alberto Paladino**

Camera: **6x6cm**

Lens: **150mm**

Film: **Kodak Ektachrome EPP ISO 100**

Exposure: **f/11**

Lighting: **Electronic flash: 3 heads**

Props and set: **Location**

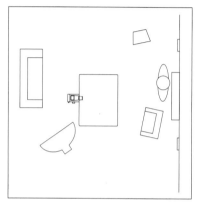

Plan View

JEANNETTE ARATA DE ERIZA

▼

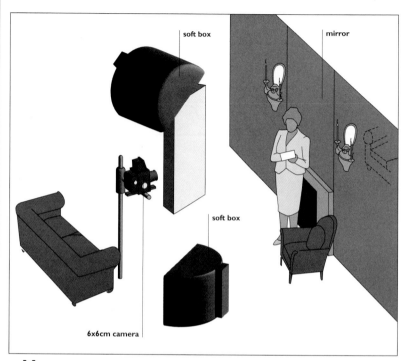

M ARIA CRISTINA WELL DESCRIBES THIS HERSELF: "THIS WAS A PART OF A CAMPAIGN FOR SWISSAIR WHERE PHOTOGRAPHERS AROUND THE WORLD WERE EACH ASKED TO CREATE AN IMAGE IN WHICH A VIP CUSTOMER LOOKED AT EASE HOLDING AN AIRLINE TICKET."

She continues: "Very soft lighting was used to flatter the looks of this extremely elegant lady. I like her reflection in the mirror, which also reflects part of her living room; this creates a mood without interfering with the main subject."

There are three lights. Because the lighting is so soft, there is no strong key. The lighting on the subject comes partly from the 75x100cm (30x40in) soft box over the camera and partly from the 45x150cm (18x60in) strip to camera left; the latter creates the slight modelling on the skirt. A third large soft box illuminates the wall opposite the mirror. Extremely careful exposure holds texture in the white suit without being too dark overall.

► *Lighting parts of a scene to be reflected in a mirror is often difficult but can be very effective*

► *Strip soft boxes can give very controllable light for "environmental" portraits of people in their surroundings*

Photographer's comment:

There were the usual problems with mirrors: you have to be very careful or you'll find some of the lighting, yourself or even the make-up artist included in the picture.

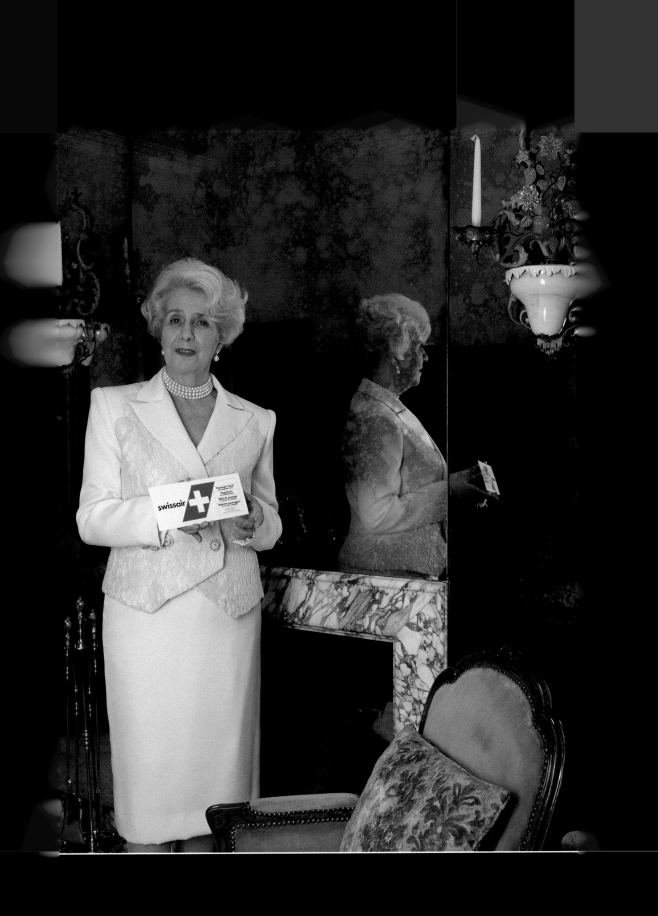

MERCEDES SOSA,
FOLK SINGER

▼

Photographer: **Maria Cristina Cassinelli**

Client: **Polygram Records**

Use: **CD cover**

Art director: **Sergio Perez Fernandez**

Camera: **6x6cm**

Lens: **150mm with Softar soft-focus screen**

Film: **Kodak TMX ISO 100**

Exposure: **1/125 second at f/11**

Lighting: **Electronic flash: 6 heads**

Props and set: **Built set**

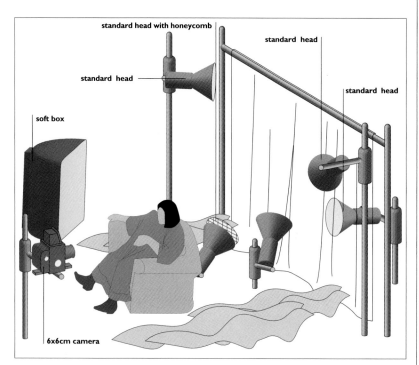

THE SINGER IS LIT WITH A SINGLE LARGE 100×200CM (40×80IN) SOFT BOX TO CAMERA LEFT. THE OTHER FIVE HEADS WERE FITTED WITH GRIDS OR SNOOTS AND WERE POSITIONED TO CREATE LIGHTS AND SHADOWS ON THE BACKGROUND.

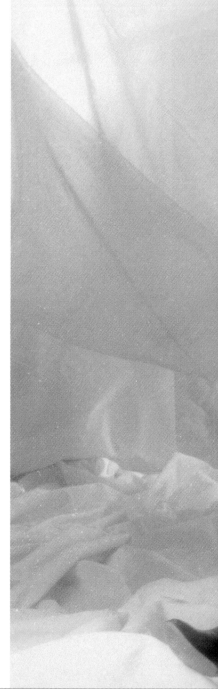

In the words of the photographer, "The set was made by a specialist, with dozens of yards of a very light fabric, covering an area of about 6x6m (20x20ft). The idea was to achieve something light, soft and romantic, to convey the mood in her songs." Because the set is unique, there is no point in describing the functions of each light in detail, but it is worth noting that they are used in a number of different ways: flat head-on illumination, transillumination, and glancing light to bring out texture. Because of the depth of the fabric, a single light might fulfil two or more of these functions: positioning of the fabric can be as important as positioning of the lights themselves.

Photographer's comment:

She has a wonderful voice, and during the shoot we had a recording of her music playing to help us with the mood.

► There are more ways of creating lightness and airiness than by simple high-key

► When using very light, trailing fabric like this, remember that even modelling lights can start a fire

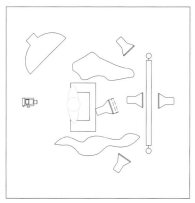

Plan View

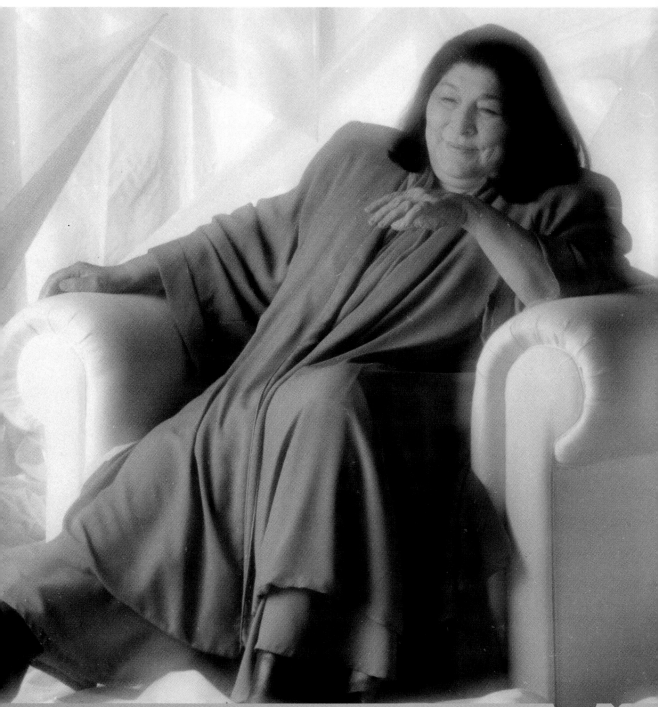

Photographer: **Stu Williamson**

Client: **Louise**

Use: **Publicity**

Camera: **6x7cm**

Lens: **150mm**

Film: **Kodak Plus-X Pan**

Exposure: **f/11**

Lighting: **Electronic flash: 2 heads**

Props and set: **Black shiny material, black
gloves, jewels, floor stand fan blowing hair**

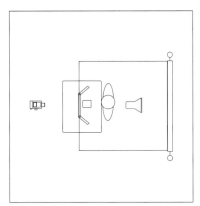

Plan View

► *A monochrome portrait does not always
have to exhibit "camera club" gradation
and skin tones*

► *Wind machines do not always have to
be used horizontally*

► *Hand colouring does not always have to
be naturalistic*

L O U I S E

▼

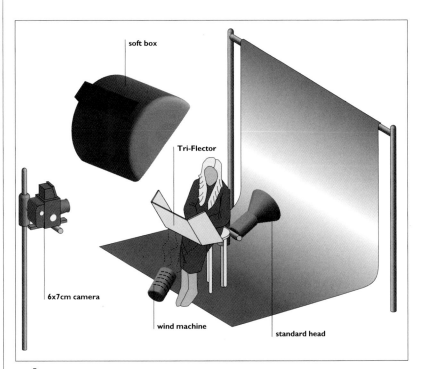

L OUISE IS A SINGER, AND THIS WAS SHOT AS A PUBLICITY PHOTOGRAPH. IT IS A GOOD
EXAMPLE OF STU WILLIAMSON'S DRAMATIC, CONTRASTY LIGHTING STYLE: A LESS ORIGINAL
PHOTOGRAPHER MIGHT NOT DARE TO "BREAK THE RULES" IN SUCH A WAY.

The reflections in the eyes reveal the
lighting. The upper reflection is of a
100x100cm (40x40in) soft box, about
100cm (40in) from the subject, above
and in front. The lower reflection is of
the Tri Flector, a three-panel reflector of
the photographer's own design; it is
more fully described on page 98.
A small light on the background

completes the set-up.

The dramatic-looking cloak is nothing
more than a length of shiny black
material; Louise was also wearing black
gloves. In the photographer's own words,
"The real key to this picture is the wind
machine, which was blowing her hair
upwards. I just shot the way the hair fell."

Photographer's comment:

*Eye contact is always important, and Louise has beautiful eyes. I coloured them yellow to
draw still more attention to them*

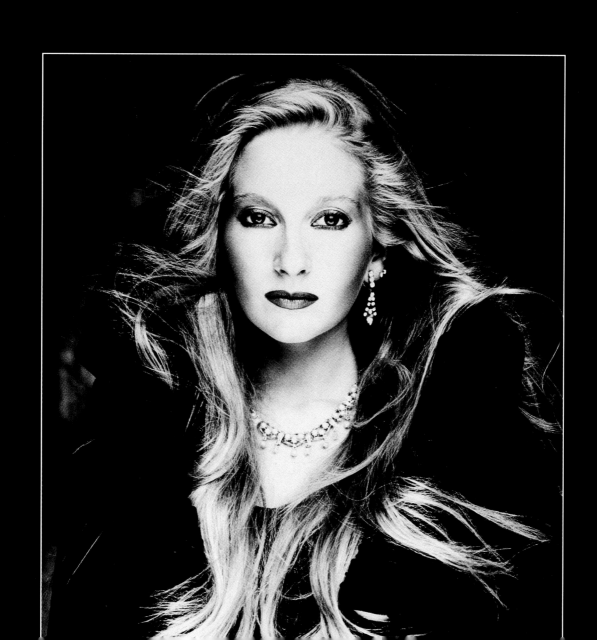

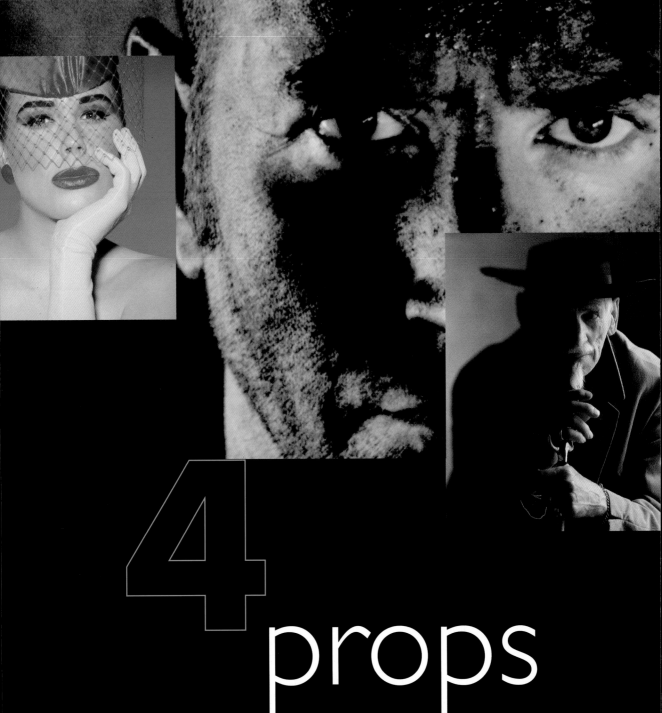

4 props

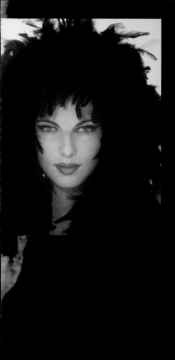

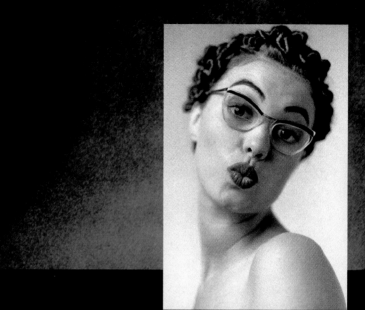

The function of a prop is to re-orient our expectations, or to tell us something about a person which we would not know without it. It can also force us to re-appraise our own attitudes: why is this amusing, why is that distressing, why is another thing erotic?

The pictures in this chapter are for the most part deliberately contrived: the photographer is telling us something which goes beyond a mere likeness of the nominal subject. He or she is creating a mystery – and, as often as not, supplying at least a part of the answer. In most of the pictures the subject stares directly at the camera, almost challenging the viewer to make something of the situation.

Often the mystery is designed to be solved by accompanying text. The aim of the portrait with props is to compel your attention, so that you want to know more about the subject. If further information is not given, the portrait can be curiously haunting: you have to project your own inventions onto it.

Backgrounds are often neutral, whether light or dark, though some are lit for texture or to complement the props, and one is effectively a set which forms a part of the props. A particularly interesting background in one shot is graded in the opposite direction from the key light, so that the lightest part of the subject stands out against the darkest part of the background, and vice versa.

Photographer: **Ben Lagunas and Alex Kuri**

Client: **Miami Magazine**

Use: **Editorial**

Model: **Cristina**

Assistant: **Isak de Ita, Janina Cohen**

Art director: **Alberto Mellini**

Stylist: **Toto**

Camera: **4x5in**

Lens: **300mm**

Film: **Kodak Tri-X Pan**

Exposure: **f/8**

Lighting: **Electronic flash: 7 heads**

Props and set: **White background**

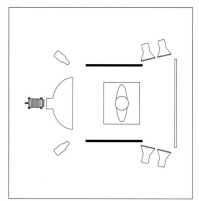

Plan View

D I V A

▼

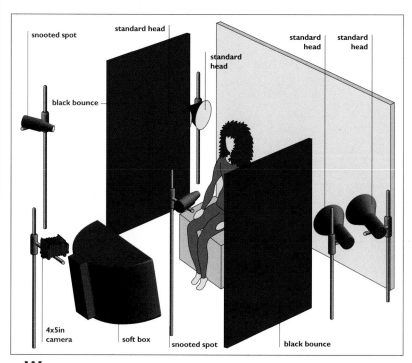

WITH A PURE WHITE BURNED-OUT BACKGROUND YOU DO NOT NEED AS MUCH SPACE BEHIND THE SUBJECT AS USUAL — BUT YOU *DO* NEED A GREAT DEAL OF LIGHT ON THE BACKGROUND, SUCH AS THE FOUR STANDARD HEADS USED HERE.

► *Dark feathers and dark fur "eat" light and require plenty of illumination if you want to show texture*

► *Very brightly illuminated high-key backgrounds will often flare through or around the edges of the subject, for good or ill*

► *High-key effects are often more dramatic in monochrome than in colour*

The three remaining lights are two snooted spots, mounted high (2m/6½ft) and symmetrically on either side of the camera, with a soft box unexpectedly mounted below and in front of the camera. Normally, lighting a portrait from below is regarded as anathema but here it is entirely logical as the soft box is only a fill: it is similar to the "troughs" of tungsten lamps which were similarly positioned in the portrait studios of yore; unlike them it does not melt the subject's make-up. Considerable amounts of light are needed to make the feathers read at all, and the model's face is at the limit of what would normally be acceptable exposure. In black and white this adds to the magic of the picture: in colour, it would probably be impossible. The lightness of the model's face is also counterbalanced by the very bright background.

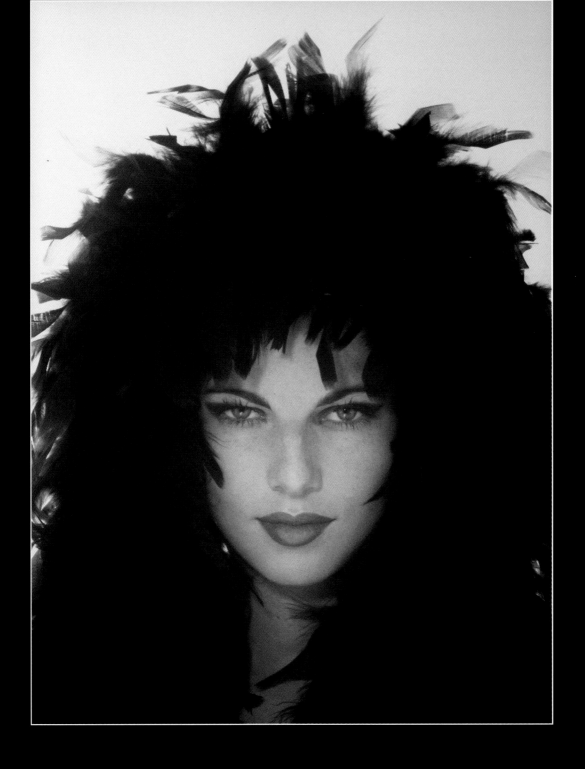

Photographer: **Lewis Lang**

Use: **Exhibition/Print Sales**

Camera: **35mm**

Lens: **28mm**

Film: **Ilford XP1 rated at EI 250**

Exposure: **Not recorded**

Lighting: **Daylight (see text)**

Props and set: **Basket of flowers; table with pedestal and statue**

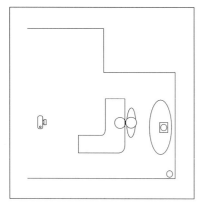

Plan View

► *The control available from opening and closing curtains and blinds (fully or partly) can be immense. Remember, this is how our ancestors' daylight studios worked*

► *Available light does not always look more natural than careful artificial lighting: the eye adapts quickly and easily to widely varying illumination levels*

M O U R N I N G   F L O W E R S

▼

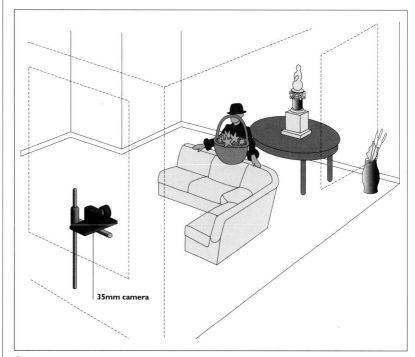

35mm camera

Lᴇᴡɪs ᴏғᴛᴇɴ ᴅᴇsᴄʀɪʙᴇs ʜɪs ᴏᴡɴ ᴘɪᴄᴛᴜʀᴇs ʙᴇsᴛ: "Dᴇ́ᴊᴀ-ᴠᴜ ᴀʟʟ ᴏᴠᴇʀ ᴀɢᴀɪɴ. … Mʏ ᴍᴀɪɴ ᴊᴏʙ ʜᴇʀᴇ ᴡᴀs ᴛᴏ ᴏᴘᴇɴ ᴜᴘ ᴛʜᴇ ᴡɪɴᴅᴏᴡ sʜᴀᴅᴇs/ᴠᴇɴᴇᴛɪᴀɴ ʙʟɪɴᴅs ᴀɴᴅ sᴀʏ 'ᴀᴀᴀʜʜʜ!' ᴛᴏ ᴛʜᴇ ʟɪɢʜᴛɪɴɢ."

The key light is in effect a large window to camera right, about 1.2–1.5m (4–5ft) from the subject. This provided soft yet directional side illumination from indirect sky-lighting. A very large, long window behind the camera provided frontal fill, again from indirect sky-lighting. This window was 3m (10ft) or more from the subject.

The white walls acted both as background and as built-in reflectors to even out and fill in the large area taken in by the wide-angle lens. Although 28mm lenses are normally associated with "violent" perspective, the strong symmetry of the composition, together with careful alignment of the camera, means that the picture "works" very well indeed. Also, the quality available from the best 35mm lenses and the best films can surprise the users of larger formats.

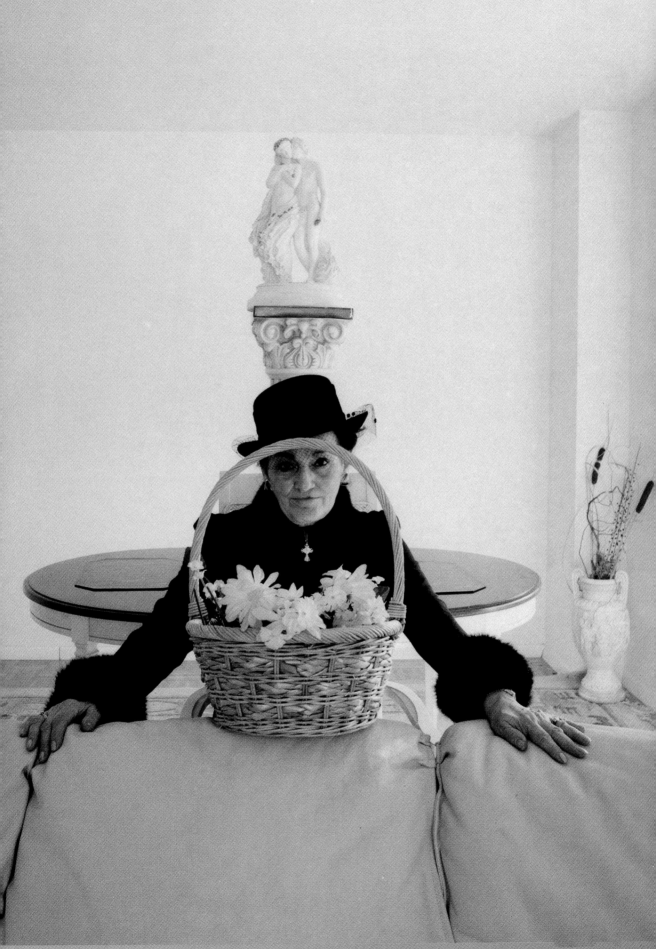

Photographer: **Peter Laqua**

Use: **Self-promotion**

Model: **Monica**

Stylist: **Silke Schöepfer**

Camera: **35mm**

Lens: **85mm**

Film: **Monochrome ISO 125/22**

Exposure: **f/1.8**

Lighting: **Electronic flash: 2 heads**

Props and set: **White paper background**

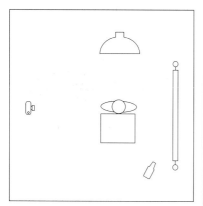

Plan View

M O N I C A

▼

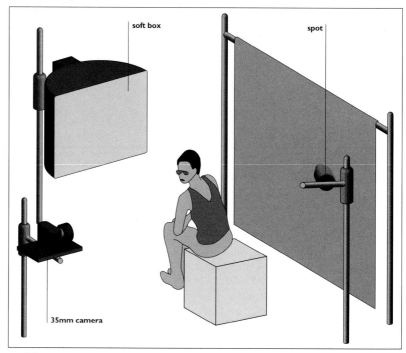

THE GLASSES, THE HAIR, THE SELF-CONSCIOUS POUT: THE EFFECT IS PURE 1950S, WITH OVERTONES OF GARY LARSEN'S *THE FAR SIDE* CARTOONS. THE HIGH-KEY EFFECT IS RENDERED THE MORE DRAMATIC BY THE DARK HAIR.

The lighting is simple enough, though the background well illustrates the need to light the background separately (and reasonably powerfully) in a high-key picture. A standard head fulfils this task.

The key light is a 100x100cm (40x40in) soft box to camera left, set slightly forward of the model's head: this provides some light even on the left side of her face, though a more conventional high-key approach would also have used a reflector to camera right to approach more closely Japanese-style notan, the antithesis to European chiaroscuro.

► *With 35mm, long lenses of wide or very wide aperture are required in order to approach the shallow depth of field our ancestors took for granted in portraits*

► *The "photo booth" simplicity of the presentation adds still more to the surrealism of the image*

Photographer's comment:

The eyes and the lips are the point of focus.

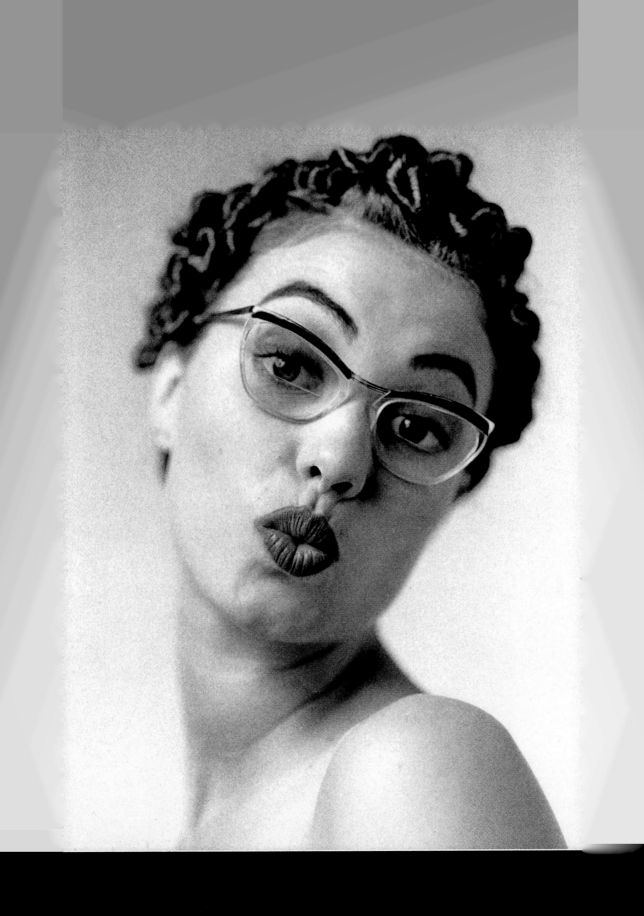

Photographer: **Frank P. Wartenberg**

Use: **Portfolio**

Camera: **6x7cm**

Lens: **185mm with warming filter**

Film: **Fuji Velvia ISO 50**

Exposure: **Not recorded (multiple exposure)**

Lighting: **Electronic flash: 4 heads**

Props and set: **Grey background paper**

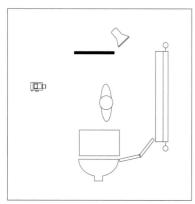

Plan View

► *The line around the head is achieved by multiple exposures with only the background lights switched on*

► *There is no such thing as correct exposure; there is only pleasing exposure*

► *With slow, contrasty films, 1/3 stop bracketing may be essential and 1/2 stop is generally the most that can be used*

C I G A R

▼

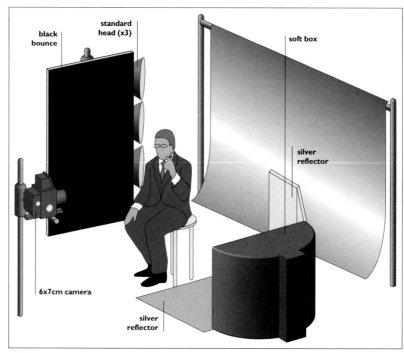

THIS IS A GOOD ILLUSTRATION OF THE "BLACK-BOUNCE" TECHNIQUE FOR DRAMATICALLY DIRECTIONAL LIGHTING — AND IT ALSO ILLUSTRATES HOW SUCCESSFUL SUCH LIGHTING CAN BE WHEN THE SOURCE IS VERY BROAD.

Three of the four heads are used to illuminate the background, which is a neutral grey; the effect of the warming (pale orange) filter is most obvious here. The fourth light is a broad soft box to camera right with two big silver reflectors, one beside it and one on the ground in front of it. The black bounce on the other side helps to kill any potential fill.

Perhaps surprisingly, the film chosen is Velvia, which is very contrasty and "punchy". On the one hand, this emphasizes the directionality of the lighting; on the other, it means that the hand holding the cigar is effectively overexposed in conventional terms, though this makes the lighting still more dramatic.

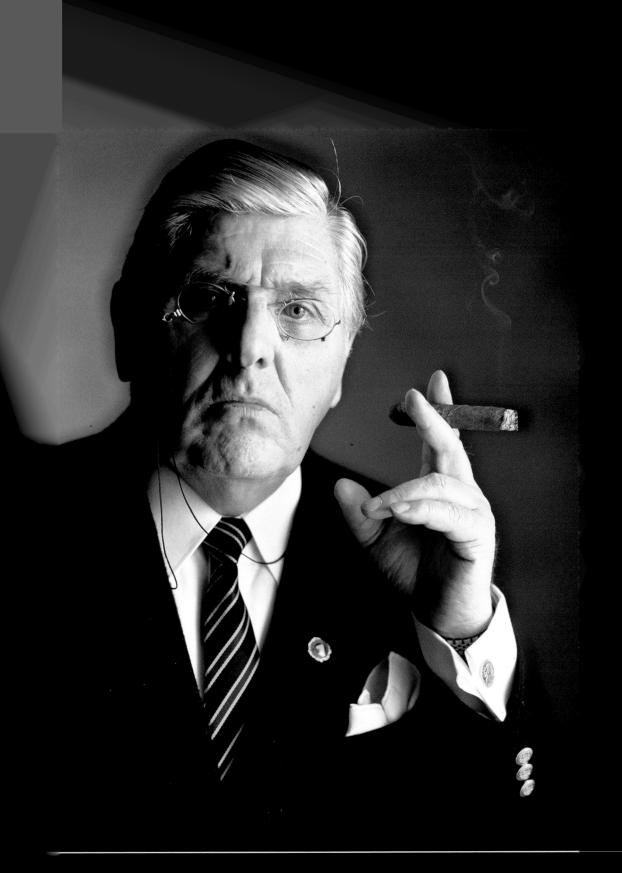

Photographer: **Frank P. Wartenberg**

Use: **Portfolio**

Camera: **35mm**

Lens: **200mm**

Film: **Polaroid Polagraph**

Exposure: **Not recorded (but see text)**

Lighting: **Tungsten: one spot**

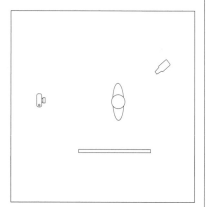

Plan View

▼

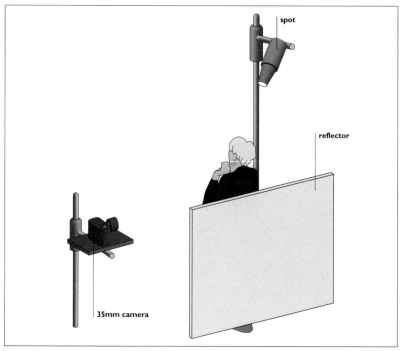

BACK LIGHTING AND A LONG EXPOSURE ARE OBVIOUSLY THE BEST WAY TO REPRESENT SMOKE, CAPTURING THE MODEL'S HAIR AT THE SAME TIME; BUT WHAT IS THE BEST WAY TO GET DETAIL IN THOSE PARTS OF THE PICTURE NEAREST THE CAMERA?

The answer in this case was silver reflectors, positioned as shown in the diagram. They throw enough light back at the subject to reduce the contrast to acceptable levels. On the one hand, black and white inherently has the ability to record a greater contrast range than colour; on the other, the film chosen was high-contrast Polaroid Polagraph rather than the less contrasty general-application Polaroid Polapan. Even so, while highlights may burn out in monochrome, there is not the often distressing loss of colour which accompanies overexposure in colour. The overall effect is one of a curiously innocent decadence, of Monte Carlo in the 1950s perhaps.

► *The length of exposure necessary to capture an image like this is unlikely to be much less than 1/4 second or much more than two or three seconds*

► *The highlights on the zip, etc, on the front of the jacket have blurred during the long exposure*

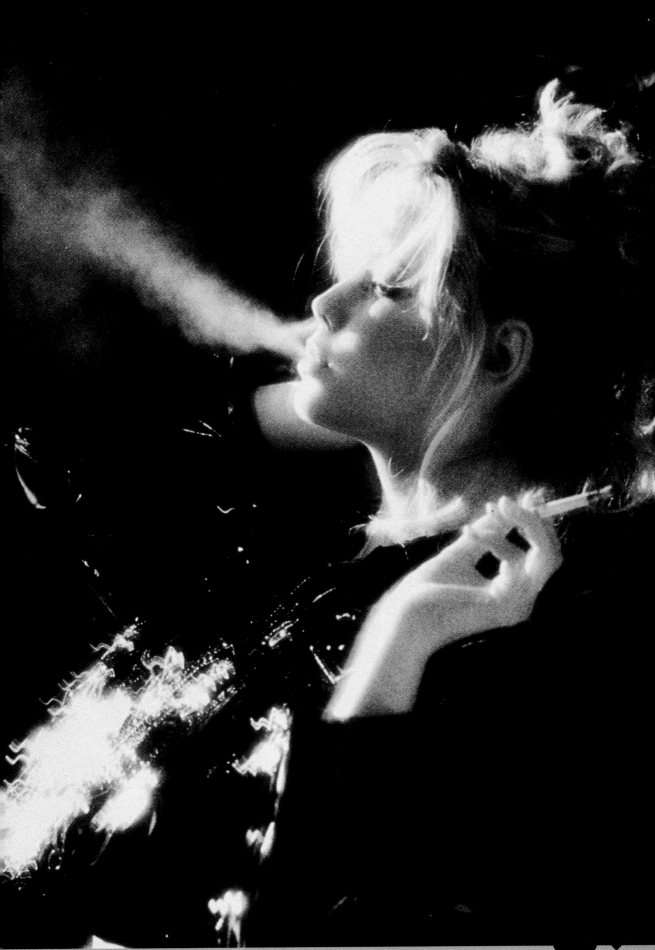

Photographer: **Frank P. Wartenberg**

Use: **Portfolio**

Camera: **35mm**

Lens: **105mm**

Film: **Polaroid Polagraph**

Exposure: **Not recorded**

Lighting: **Electronic flash: 2 heads**

Props and set: **Net, black background**

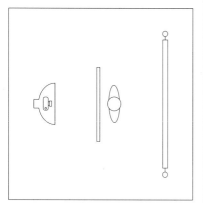

Plan View

▼

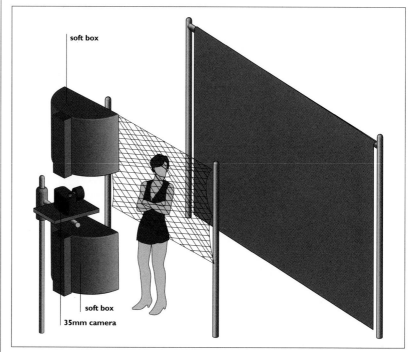

soft box

soft box

35mm camera

WHAT YOU SEE IS WHAT YOU GET. THE NET WAS STRETCHED BETWEEN TWO SUPPORTS; THE BACKGROUND IS BLACK PAPER; AND THE VERY FLAT, EVEN LIGHTING IS FROM TWO SOFT BOXES, ONE ABOVE AND ONE BELOW THE CAMERA.

Frank Wartenberg is one of a number of photographers who has explored high-contrast Polagraph film which is not intended for general photography, and this is a good example of the gap between idea and execution. Once you have the idea – which could come from something seen by chance, or via a more analytical process – you have to find the right kind of net; learn how to damage it in just the right way in order to get the sort of hole you want; work out how to support it; devise lighting which is soft enough not to cast shadows from the net onto the subject's face; and then compose it just right – note the way in which the model's eyebrow obscures the upper part of the rent.

► *Working to realize a previsualized idea is one of the finest ways to learn new techniques and improve old skills*

► *A good time to experiment is after you have already got the paid-for shot "in the can"; then you can play around with the same picture elements*

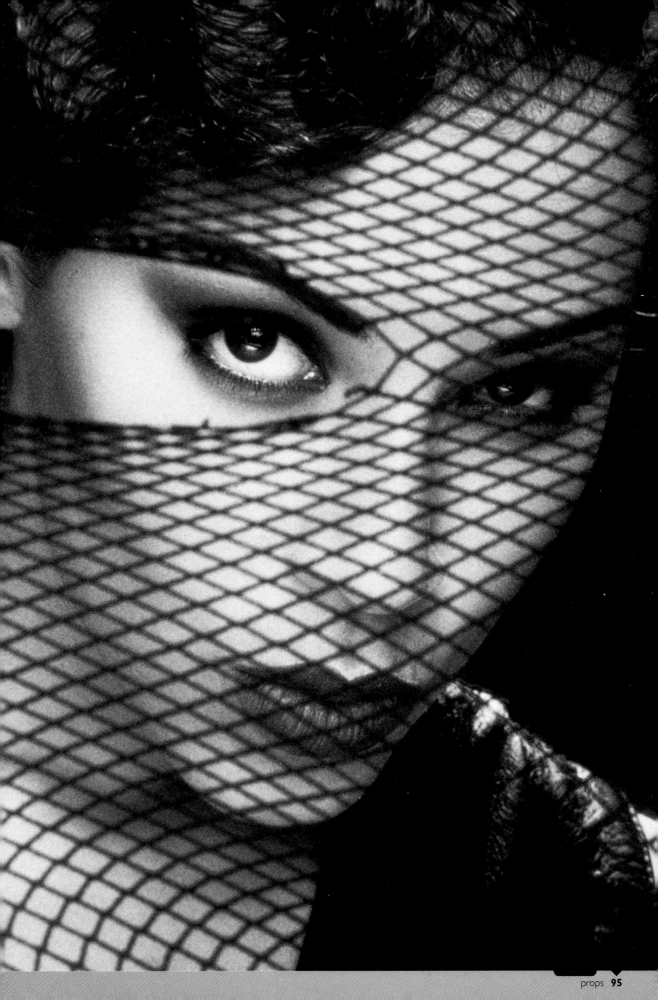

Photographer: **Frank P. Wartenberg**

Use: **Portfolio**

Camera: **6x7cm**

Lens: **185mm + light orange filter**

Film: **Fuji Velvia**

Exposure: **Not recorded; probably about f/5.6**

Lighting: **Electronic flash: 4 heads**

Props and set: **Grey background paper**

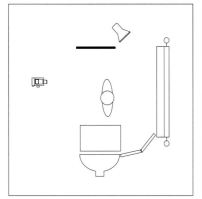

Plan View

▼

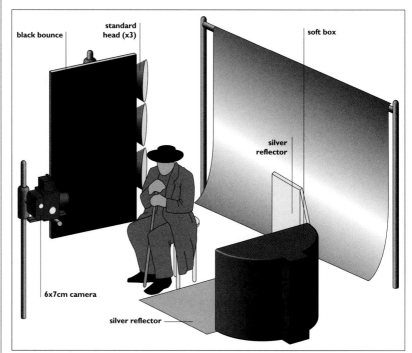

black bounce

standard head (x3)

soft box

silver reflector

silver reflector

6x7cm camera

STRONGLY DIRECTIONAL LIGHTING IS OFTEN VERY SUCCESSFUL WHEN PHOTOGRAPHING PEOPLE WHO ARE NO LONGER IN THE FIRST FLUSH OF YOUTH – THOUGH MEN ARE NORMALLY MORE WILLING TO ACCEPT "CHARACTER" PORTRAITS THAN WOMEN.

The subject is very slightly back lit from camera right by a large soft box supplemented with silver reflectors, so illumination is much stronger to camera right than to camera left: a black bounce kills any reflections which might act as a fill on the right side of the subject's face.

The background is lit with three heads to provide a graded ground which is darker to camera right and lighter to camera left, thereby making the subject stand out all the more clearly. For the initial exposure, both the soft box and the background lights were on; for several subsequent exposures, only the background lights were on; this produced the black shadow around the head and the softness of the outline.

► *Lighting the subject from one side, and grading the background from the other, can be very effective*

► *The larger the format, the better it will "see into the shadows"*

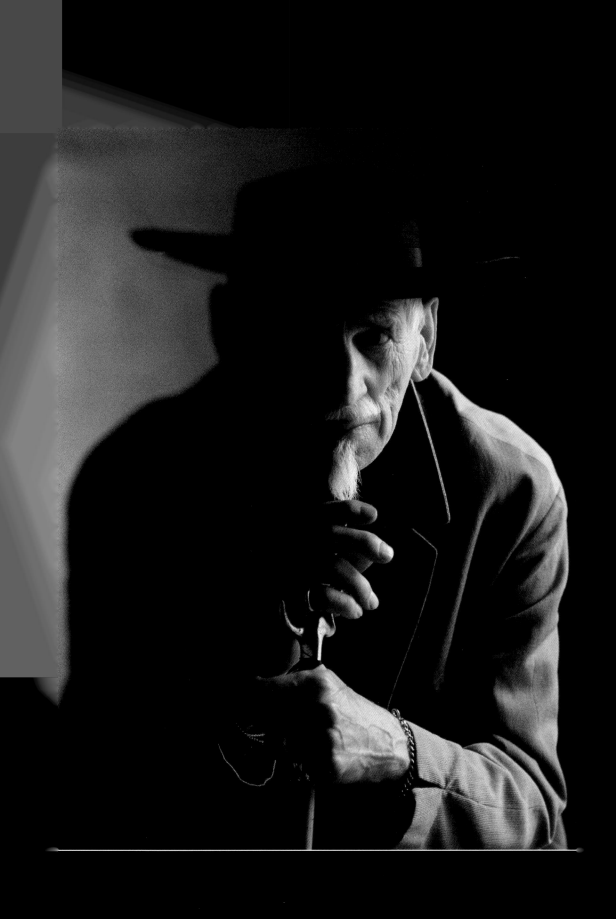

Photographer: **Stu Williamson**

Client: **Terry English**

Use: **Editorial,** *Arms and Armour* **magazine**

Model: **Angie Dickinson**

Camera: **6x7cm**

Lens: **150mm**

Film: **Kodak T-Max 100**

Exposure: **f/11**

Lighting: **Electronic flash: 2 heads**

Props and set: **Painted background**

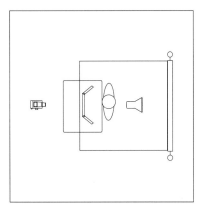

Plan View

▼

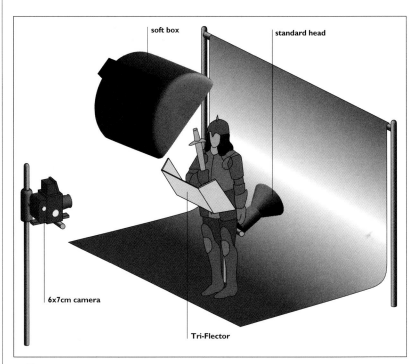

soft box · standard head · 6x7cm camera · Tri-Flector

I N THE LATE 20TH CENTURY FEW PHOTOGRAPHERS HAVE THE OPPORTUNITY TO SHOOT WHAT IS IN EFFECT AN ADVERTISING PHOTOGRAPH FOR A WORKING ARMOURER; AND FEWER STILL WOULD CHOOSE SUCH A MOODY REPRESENTATION.

The photograph owes at least as much to the Tri-Flector, a three-section reflector of the photographer's own design, as to the lighting. There is a small spot on the background, and the key light on the subject is a 100x100cm (40x40in) soft box about a metre (3¼ft) away, in front of and above the model's head. Use of the Tri-Flector (which is commercially produced by Lastolite in Britain) is almost a trade-mark of Stu's photographic style. It consists of a central portion with two "wings" which can be angled upwards to varying degrees. It is positioned just out of shot below the field of view of the camera, and reflects the light from the key back up at the subject.

► *The Tri-Flector is effectively a focusing reflector, so the fill is much more intense than you would get from a flat reflector*

► *Metal armour (and other shiny materials) can reflect darkness as easily as light*

Photographer's comment:

The sword in the picture is the one which "starred" in the movie Excalibur.

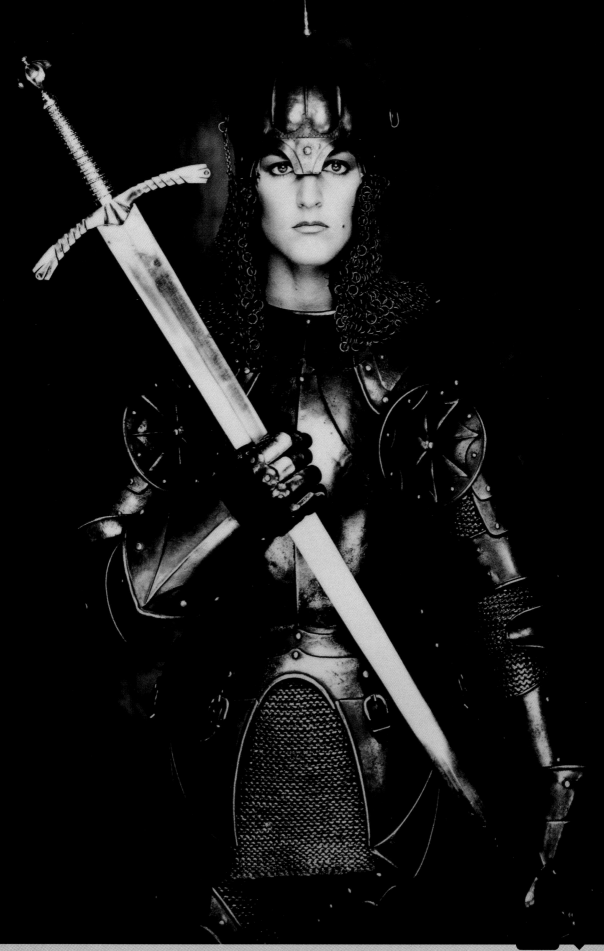

Photographer: **Johnny Boylan**

Client: **S.M.I./Powergen**

Use: **Advertising**

Assistant: **Siri Hills**

Art director: **Roy Brooks**

Camera: **4x5in**

Lens: **210mm**

Film: **Agfa APX 100**

Exposure: **f/8; shutter speed not recorded**

Lighting: **Mixed flash and tungsten**

Props and set: **Painted backdrop, timber**

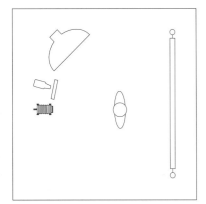

Plan View

M I N E R

▼

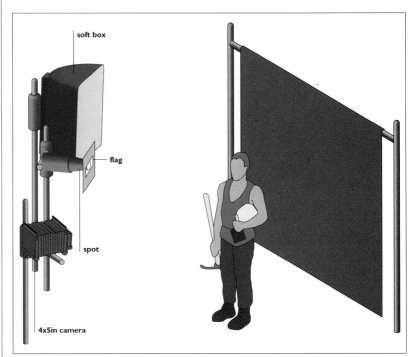

THERE IS A VARIETY OF PORTRAIT, UNUSUAL TODAY, WHICH WAS POPULAR WITH OUR VICTORIAN ANCESTORS. IT IS EFFECTIVELY A CROSS BETWEEN REPORTAGE AND THE FORMAL PORTRAIT. THE OVERALL EFFECT CAN BE VERY POWERFUL.

Such pictures were shot both on location and in the studio, and some 19th-century shots may seem contrived today, but they are always distinguished by what is to modern eyes an exquisite level of detail – a consequence of the large formats employed. Johnny Boylan followed in this tradition by using a 4x5in camera and his favourite Agfa APX film.

The lighting recreates the harsh light of a mine in an unexpected way. The key is arguably the big soft box to camera left, slightly in front of the subject, but a great deal of the impact comes from the direct, almost challenging stare. The eyes were lit separately, with a 2K tungsten lamp flagged down to a letterbox slot directly above the camera.

► *Large formats not only render detail well; they also have an ability to "see into the shadows" which is unequalled by smaller formats*

► *In a built set a very skilled make-up artist is usually necessary to make the scene convincing*

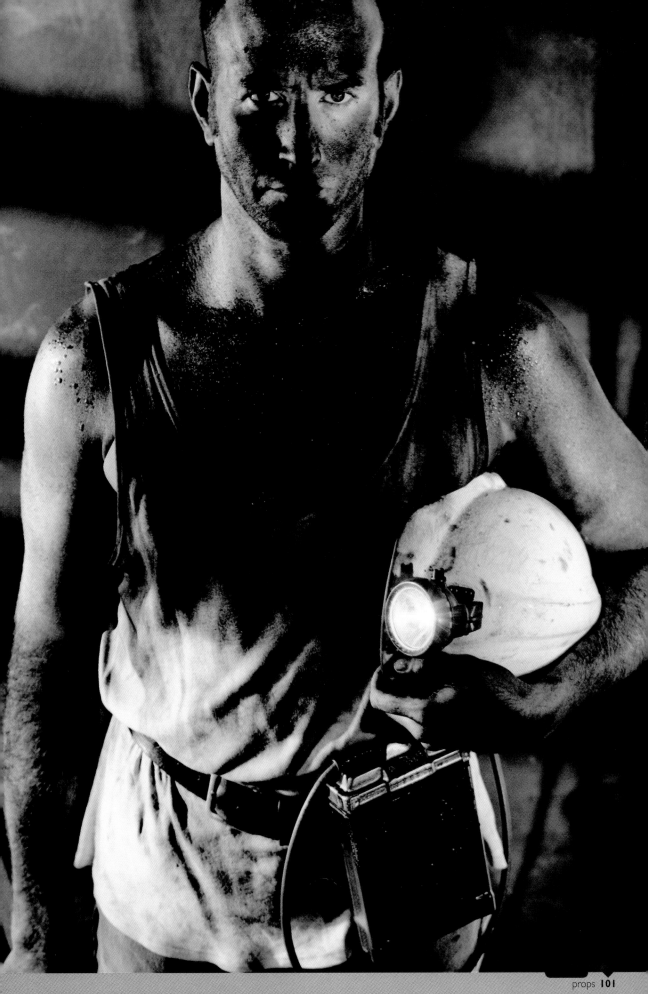

▼

Photographer: **Struan**

Client: **Ilford Cibachrome**

Use: **Publicity/advertising**

Model: **Kate Cummins**

Assistant: **James Fraser**

Make-up: **Steve Marine**

Art director: **Peter Holmes**

Camera: **35mm**

Lens: **105mm**

Film: **Kodachrome 64**

Exposure: **f/8**

Lighting: **Electronic flash: 2 heads**

Props and set: **Blue background; hat made from red satin; yellow gloves**

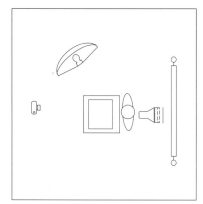

Plan View

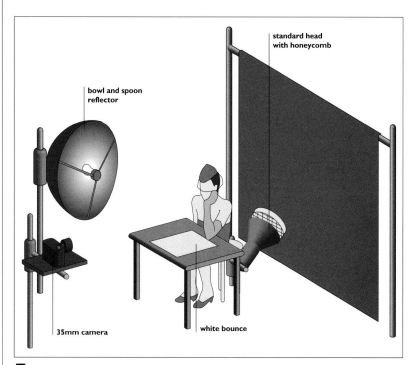

standard head with honeycomb

bowl and spoon reflector

35mm camera

white bounce

THIS WAS SHOT TO SHOW WHAT ILFORD CIBACHROME REVERSAL PRINTING MATERIAL COULD DO, WITH PURE, BRIGHT COLOURS AND TRUE-TO-LIFE FLESH TONES. CIBACHROME IS NOW KNOWN AS ILFOCHROME CLASSIC; IT REMAINS THE PREMIUM MATERIAL FOR POS/POS PRINTING.

The only light on the model is a large-diameter shallow reflector of the type sometimes known as a "bowl and spoon"; this gives a much more directional light than a soft box, but still very broad and even. It is directly over the camera, and gives the single catch-light in the model's eyes.

Her arm is resting on a table, just for comfort, so the photographer placed a white card on the table to provide a little fill: look at the underside of the glove. The background is lit with a honeycombed spot, with a blue gel to intensify the colour of the blue paper more. It is angled so as to grade the tone.

► *Prop hunting and professional make-up are as much a part of photography as cameras and lighting*

► *Very precise exposure is necessary to extract maximum saturation without making the image unnaturally dark*

Photographer's comment:

Even though Cibachrome was an Ilford product, they didn't have a slide film of their own at the time, so I used Kodachrome for maximum saturation. We made the hat, and those were the only long, yellow gloves we could find. The make-up is of course taken to the limit.

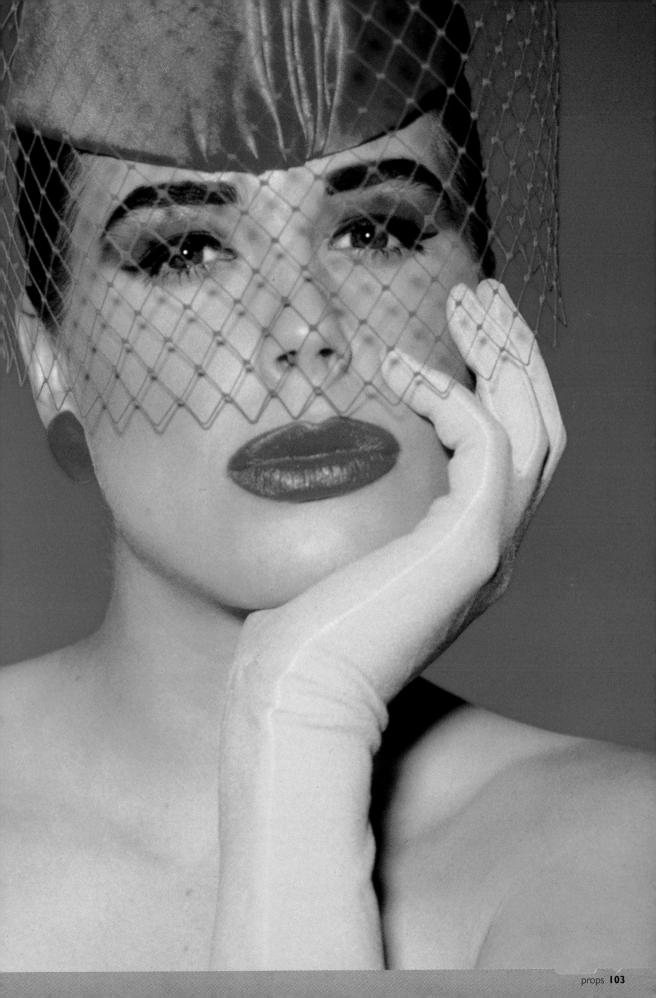

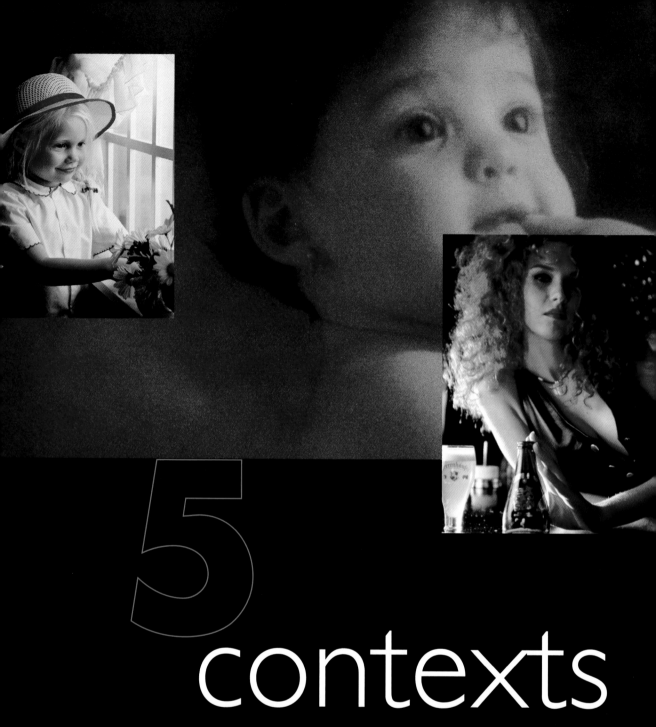

5

contexts

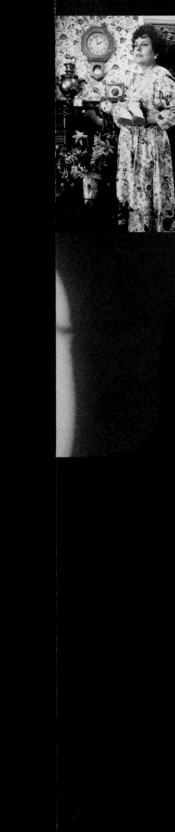

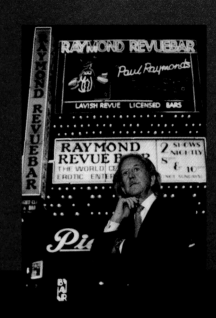

► Once again, the dividing line between this chapter, Contexts, and the preceding one, Props, is far from clear. The difference is principally one of scale, though there is also the point that you could remove the people from most of these pictures and you would have a built set or location which was begging to have a person in it. In the previous chapter, the pictures would not really exist without a person in them.

The techniques of lighting are similar to those used in previous chapters, except that there is often a need to light quite a large area in order to show the context clearly. As ever, this does not mean that the lighting is necessarily flat: rather, it means that the overall lighting ratio should normally be close enough, so that the appropriate tonal ranges in both the subject and the background can be captured adequately on the film. Strictly, colour film can capture at least as wide a tonal range as monochrome, but it can hold acceptable colours within that tonal range only across three or four stops: anything lighter tends to wash out to an unpleasant yellow; anything darker is represented by shades of grey or brown.

Photographer: **Dolors Porredon**

Client: **Studio**

Use: **Poster**

Camera: **6x6cm**

Lens: **150mm**

Film: **Kodak Vericolor III**

Exposure: **f/8**

Lighting: **Electronic flash: single soft box**

Props and set: **Built set**

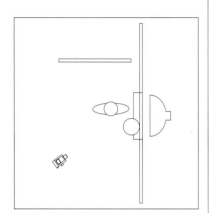

Plan View

N I Ñ A   D E T R A S   D E   L A   V E N T A N A

▼

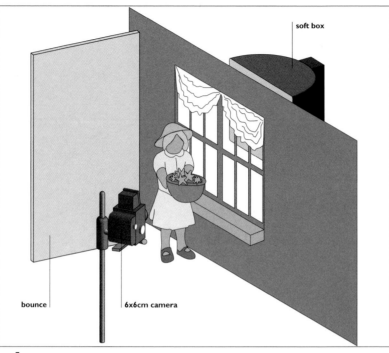

soft box

bounce

6x6cm camera

A PERFECT MOMENT, CAPTURED BY CHANCE – OR CAREFUL PLANNING? THE LATTER, OF COURSE. THE WINDOW IS PART OF A BUILT SET, TRANSILLUMINATED WITH A 100×100CM (40×40IN) SOFT BOX, SUPPLEMENTED ONLY BY A WHITE BOUNCE TO CAMERA LEFT.

▶ *Soft yet directional lighting is often very effective with children*

▶ *Flash is usually best for children, as they may screw up their eyes against tungsten lighting*

▶ *Some photographers believe that flash can damage the eyes of young children, but there is absolutely no evidence to support this: it seems to be an old wives' tale*

Although this was designed for a poster, the same techniques (and forethought, and organization) could equally be applied to a picture for less public consumption. Window sets are not particularly hard to build; a selection of hats can be kept at hand; the rest of the clothing is hardly elaborate, though the light colour emphasizes purity and innocence; and the lighting is elegantly simple. It is true that, often, surprisingly complex lighting set-ups are used to mimic simplicity; but it is also true that a simple lighting set-up can (if it is well executed) be remarkably effective. Diffuse light generally works very well with children, emphasizing the delicacy of their skin texture and the roundness of their features: "character" lighting is considerably more difficult before the features have reached their adult lineaments.

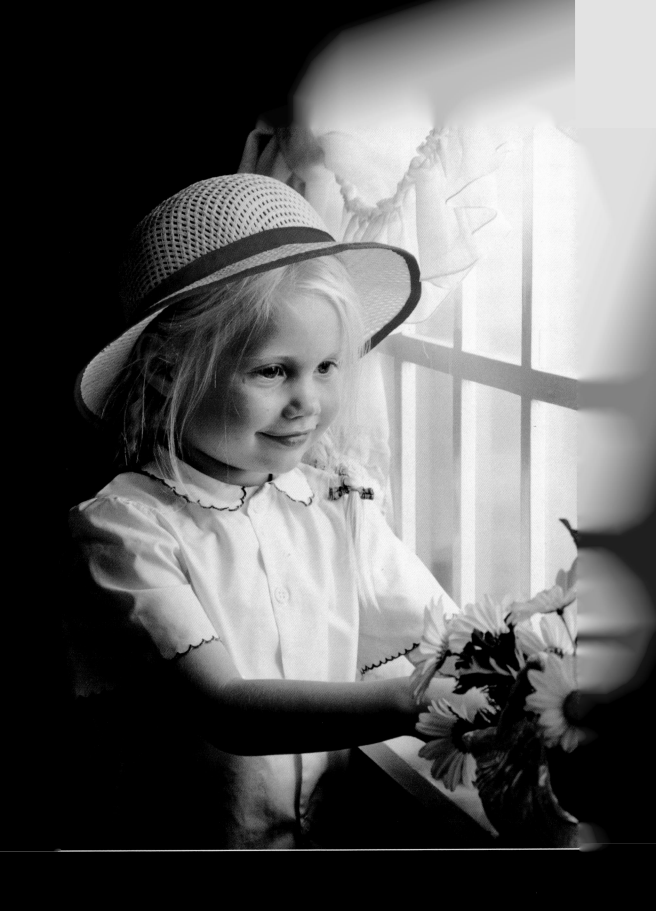

Photographer: **Dolors Porredon**

Client: **Studio**

Use: **Poster**

Camera: **6x6cm**

Lens: **150mm + 81A filter**

Film: **Kodak Vericolor III**

Exposure: **f/5.6**

Lighting: **Electronic flash: 1 soft box, filtered**

Props and set: **Chestnut/beige background**

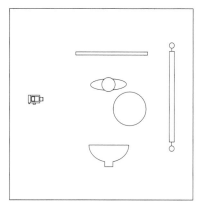

Plan View

► *Some parents (and most grandparents) will be delighted with nude portraits of small children. Others will find the idea disquieting*

► *Keep the studio warm if you want to photograph babies or toddlers in the nude. The children probably won't care, but the parents will*

► *Warm colours, and even warm-filtered light, often complement the colours and textures of bare skin*

S U E Ñ O S   I N F A N T I L E S

▼

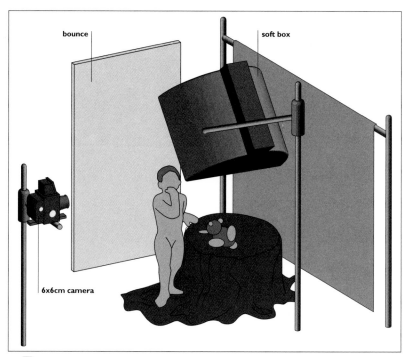

bounce

soft box

6x6cm camera

T HERE ARE SOME PHOTOGRAPHERS WHO SEEMINGLY PRODUCE WITH EASE THE KIND OF PICTURES WHICH OTHERS ATTEMPT — AND FAIL TO ACHIEVE. EVERYONE HAS SEEN A HUNDRED BAD IMITATIONS OF THIS SORT OF PICTURE: FEW CAN PRODUCE THE IDEAL.

The lighting, as with so many of Dolors Porredon's pictures, is simplicity itself: a single 80x80cm (32x32in) soft box to camera right, supplemented with a bounce to camera left. The light from the soft box is warmed with a beige gel, and the whole image is warmed still further with an 81A filter on the camera lens. That is all; but the light is in precisely the right place, with precisely the right fill, and with carefully chosen props and background.

In the present climate of opinion, it is inadvisable to photograph children much older than this in the nude: what some see as charming innocence, others see as "child porn". Even at this age, the sex of the child should not be too apparent from the picture.

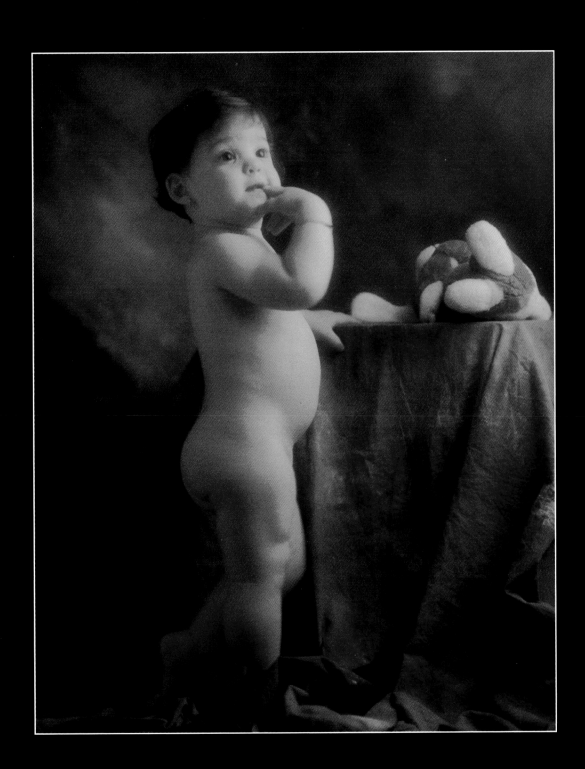

Photographer: **Lewis Lang**

Use: **Exhibition/print sales**

Model: **"My mom"**

Camera: **35mm**

Lens: **28mm**

Film: **Fujipan 1600 at EI 1000**

Exposure: **Not recorded**

Lighting: **Available: daylight plus tungsten**

Props and set: **Assembled from available materials**

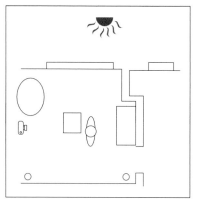

Plan View

WALLFLOWER

▼

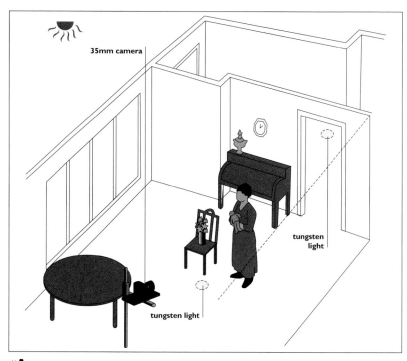

"**A**VAILABLE LIGHT" IS A RELATIVE TERM. THIS WAS SHOT IN LEWIS LANG'S MOTHER'S KITCHEN. HE PULLED BACK THE TRANSLUCENT CURTAINS COVERING THE KITCHEN WINDOWS, AND TURNED ON THE TUNGSTEN LIGHTS SHOWN IN THE DIAGRAM.

► *One of the great advantages of monochrome with available light (and modified available light) is that you can mix daylight and tungsten with impunity*

► *Very small self-slave flash units can be useful for modifying the lighting in interiors*

► *Films with extended red sensitivity may give a slight infrared effect under tungsten light unless they are used with the weakest available blue filter*

The four kitchen windows to camera left were each about 150x60cm (5x2ft) tall and wide and were about 2.2–3m (7–10ft) from the subject. The light coming through them was indirect sunlight, from open sky. A tungsten lamp to camera left (out of shot, alongside the camera) provided extra fill, as did two tungsten lights built into the ceiling to camera right; the further lamp at the right also added some "kicker" top/back-lighting to the woman's hair. Beyond the backdrop wall, a glass-panelled front door provided some fill in the foyer seen through the kitchen door to the right.

Skilled use of "available light" (modified with curtains, etc, as seen here) reminds us how our ancestors could achieve such good results in their daylight studios, always lit by indirect windowlighting.

Photographer's comment:

Home is where the light is. I especially like simple lighting when it enhances the subject. The incongruous sneakers add a humorous note.

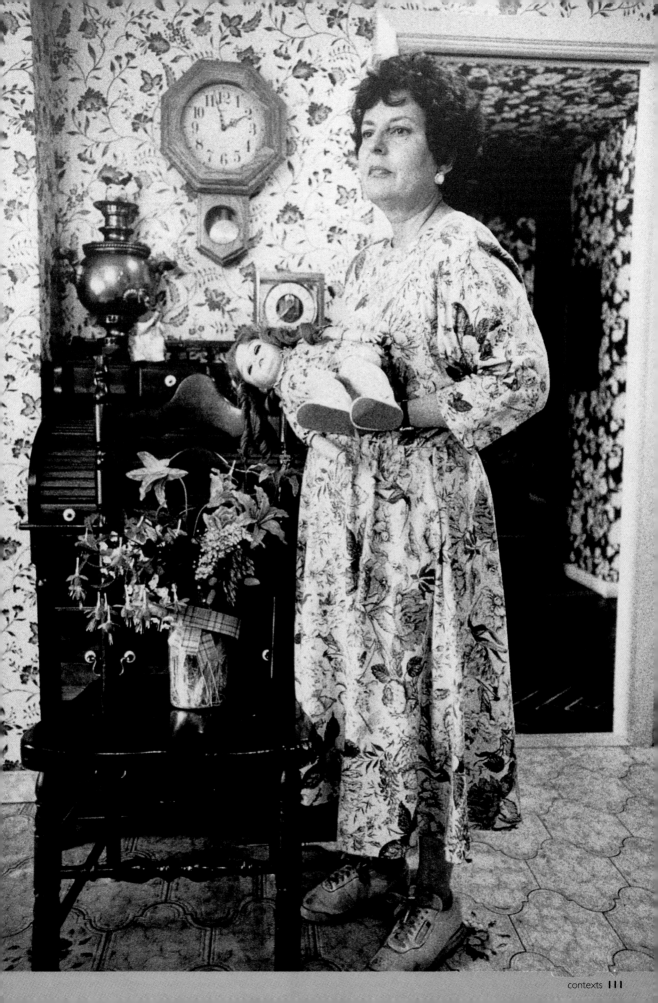

Photographer: **Terry Ryan**

Client: **Symphony Hall**

Art director: **Malcolm Davis**

Camera: **6x6cm**

Lens: **120mm macro**

Film: **Kodak Ektachrome 100 Plus**

Exposure: **1/250 second at f/11**

Lighting: **Electronic flash: 2 heads**

Props and set: **Location**

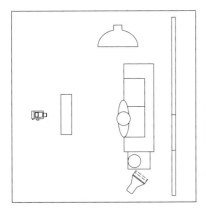

Plan View

CARLO MARIA GIULINI, CONDUCTOR

▼

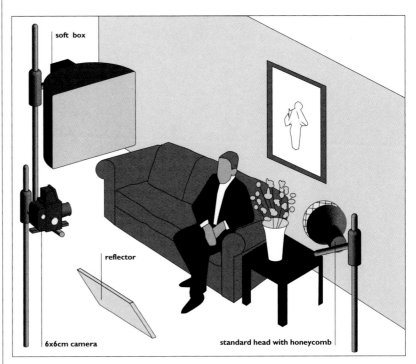

As WITH SO MANY PICTURES WHICH LOOK AS IF THEY WERE TAKEN BY UNUSUALLY FELICITOUS AVAILABLE LIGHT, THIS PICTURE IS IN FACT QUITE CAREFULLY LIT WITH TWO HEADS — ONE OF WHICH ILLUMINATES THE PORTRAIT OF THE CONDUCTOR ON THE WALL BEHIND HIM.

The key light is a 90x90cm (3x3ft) soft box with 1600 joules of light to camera left. This is supplemented by a Lastolite folding reflector below the subject's knees, throwing some light back up to lower the contrast, particularly important when, as here, the subject is wearing a dark suit and a white shirt.

The other light, on the background, is a 500 joule standard head to camera right; it is honeycombed to reduce spill, and to obviate having two catch-lights in the subject's eyes. There is also sunlight coming through a window to camera right: it is this which casts the shadows of the flowers.

► *Without the background light, the portrait on the wall would be unhappily bisected by a line of light and would not read well at all*

► *The face is arguably slightly overexposed, but this adds to the light, sunny, even joyful mood of the picture*

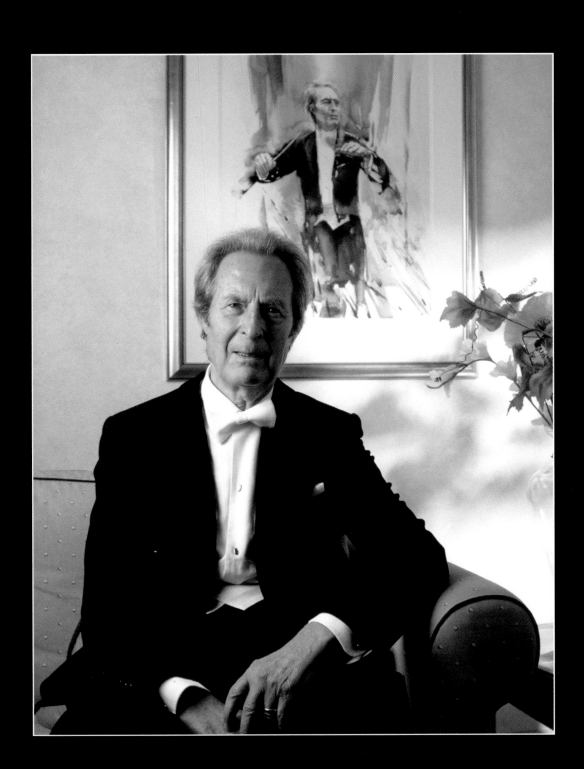

Photographer: **Maurizio Polverelli**

Client: **Explosion**

Use: **Advertising**

Model: **Barbara**

Assistant: **Emanuela Mazzoti**

Stylist: **Giovanni (IDEA 2)**

Camera: **645**

Lens: **150mm + soft focus screen**

Film: **Kodak EPR ISO 64**

Exposure: **Not recorded**

Lighting: **Electronic flash: 2 heads**

Props and set: **Location: Bounty pub in Rimini (Italy)**

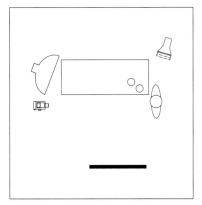

Plan View

► *Often, lighting should conform to the rule of Occam's Razor: do not multiply lights without good cause*

► *The right exposure from an aesthetic point of view is not always the same as the exposure which catches the widest tonal range*

E X P L O S I O N

▼

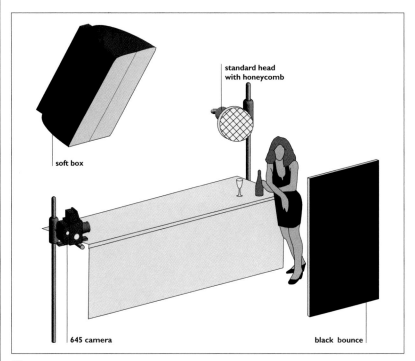

soft box

standard head with honeycomb

645 camera

black bounce

T HE BOTTLE IS THE TRUE SUBJECT — IT IS THE EXPLOSION OF THE TITLE — SO THE GIRL AND ALL THE SURROUNDINGS ARE STRICTLY PROPS. THEY DO HOWEVER FULFIL THE CLASSICAL ADVERTISING REQUIREMENT OF SAYING, "THIS IS THE KIND OF PERSON WHO DRINKS OUR PRODUCT."

The lighting is simple enough: a 50×100cm (20×40in) soft box from the front, alongside the camera, and a honeycomb spot from camera left, slightly back lighting the model's hair and more dramatically back lighting the bottle. The honeycomb spot is the true key in terms of where the shadows lie, but the label on the bottle would hardly be legible without the fill. A black bounce to camera right keeps the contrast high. In conventional terms, some parts of the right-hand side of the picture are simply overexposed; but the overall effect well recreates the interior of a pub on a hot day, when it offers a cool, shady retreat and a refreshing drink, and the soft-focus screen further recalls the difficulty one's eyes may have in adjusting after the glare outside.

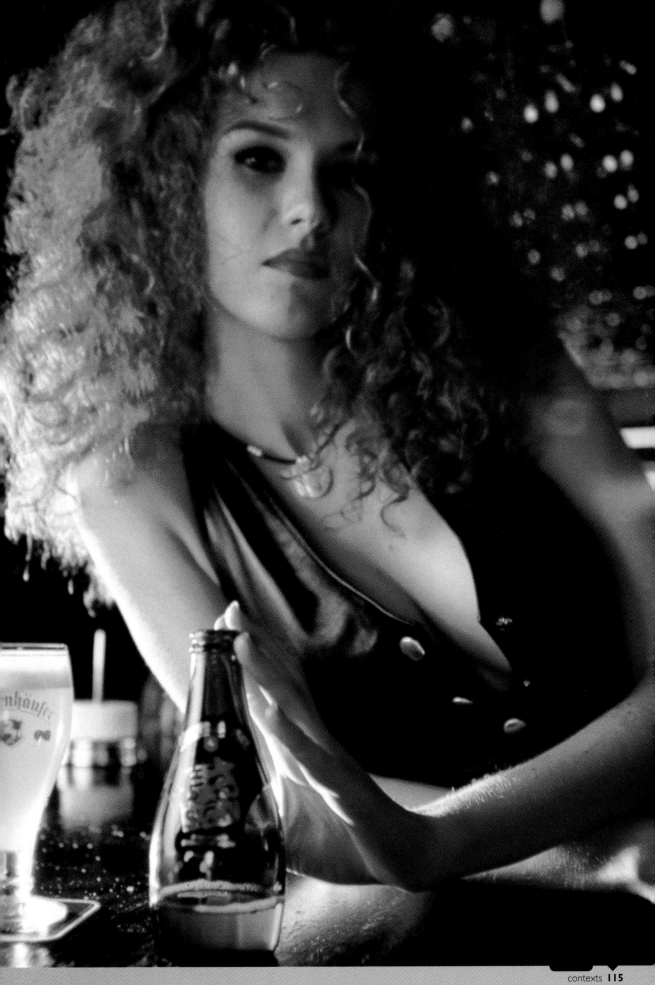

Photographer: **Johnny Boylan**

Client: *Sunday Telegraph* **Magazine**

Use: **Editorial**

Subject: **Paul Raymond**

Assistant: **Siri Hills**

Camera: **6x7cm**

Lens: **127mm**

Film: **Kodak Tri-X rated at EI 200**

Exposure: **1/15 at f/11**

Lighting: **Electronic flash plus available light**

Props and set: **Location**

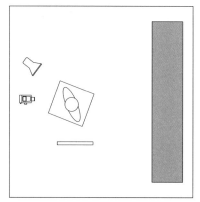

Plan View

▼

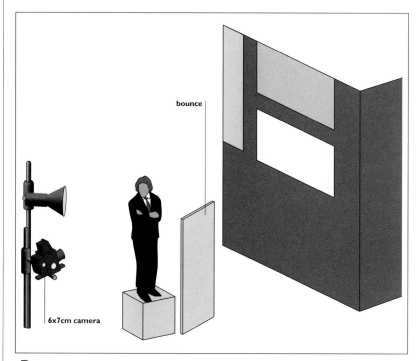

bounce

6x7cm camera

RAYMOND'S REVUEBAR AND ITS PROPRIETOR PAUL RAYMOND ARE SOHO LANDMARKS. THE CHALLENGES HERE WERE, FIRST, TO SHOW BOTH TOGETHER IN A WAY THAT SHOWED AS MUCH AS POSSIBLE OF THE REVUEBAR, AND, SECOND, TO BALANCE THE LIGHTING.

The obvious approach would have been to use a wide-angle, but that would have reduced the impact of the Revuebar itself. Equally, too long a focal length would have led to depth of field problems. A 127mm lens on a 6x7cm camera provided a useful compromise, but Mr Raymond had to stand on a milk-crate to allow precisely the right angle. Because it is so recognizable, and because all the print is so large, the Revuebar could be left to go slightly soft. This set-up required more power than would readily have been available from small, portable flash, so a studio flash unit with a long extension cable was used. It was mounted high and to camera left, while an assistant with a Lastolite collapsible white bounce stood just out of shot to camera right to provide some fill on the left side of the subject's face.

► *Any slight movement by Mr Raymond during the 1/15 second exposure would be insignificant compared with the flash exposure which "freezes" him*

► *In pictures like this you have to decide which compromises to make on composition, sharpness and lighting*

Photographer's comment:

The power cable to the flash snaked into a nearby sex club. I had fun plugging it in.

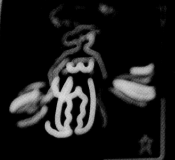

RAYMOND REVUEBAR

Paul Raymonds

LAVISH REVUE   LICENSED BARS

RAYMOND
REVUE B R
THE WORLD CE
EROTIC ENTER

2 SHOWS
NIGHTLY
8ᵖᵐ
& 10ᵖᵐ
(NOT SUNDAYS)

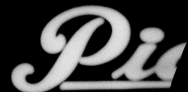

Photographer: **Peter Goodrum**

Use: **Portfolio**

Model: **Steve**

Camera: **4x5in**

Lens: **210mm**

Film: **Polaroid Type 55 P/N**

Exposure: **1/15 second at f/5.6**

Lighting: **Daylight: window 3.5m (12ft) away**

Props and set: **Engraving plate**

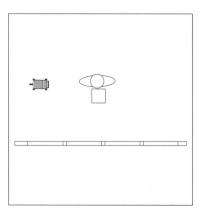

Plan View

▼

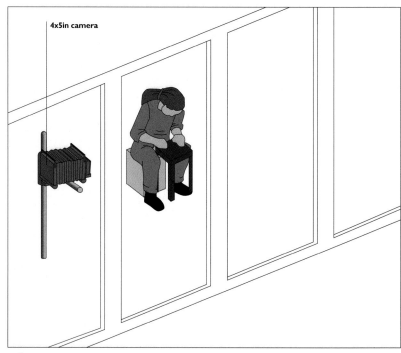

4x5in camera

AN ARTIST'S STUDIO REQUIRES A GOOD NORTH LIGHT — AND THE SITTER WAS MAKING AN ENGRAVING PLATE IN A BIG STUDIO WITH WINDOWS 2M (6½FT) OR SO HIGH AND 8–10M (26–32FT) LONG.

Even though the subject was 3.5–4.5m (12–15ft) from the window, this allowed a reasonable 1/15 second exposure at f/5.6 even on slow (ISO 50) Polaroid Type 55 P/N, which affords both a positive and a negative. The negative was printed on Kentmere Art Classic, processed in Rayco chemicals then toned with Rayco Seltone selenium toner. The finished print was then hand-coloured using Zig graphic ink markers and Daler watercolour pencils. The markers work better in the highlights, while the watercolour pencils have more body for colouring the darker tones. The overall effect is clearly hand-worked, yet equally clearly photographic in origin.

► *Kentmere Art Classic (available from Luminos in the United States) is an unusual paper without a baryta coating or paper whiteners*

► *Hand colouring can be both naturalistic and deliberately exaggerated at the same time*

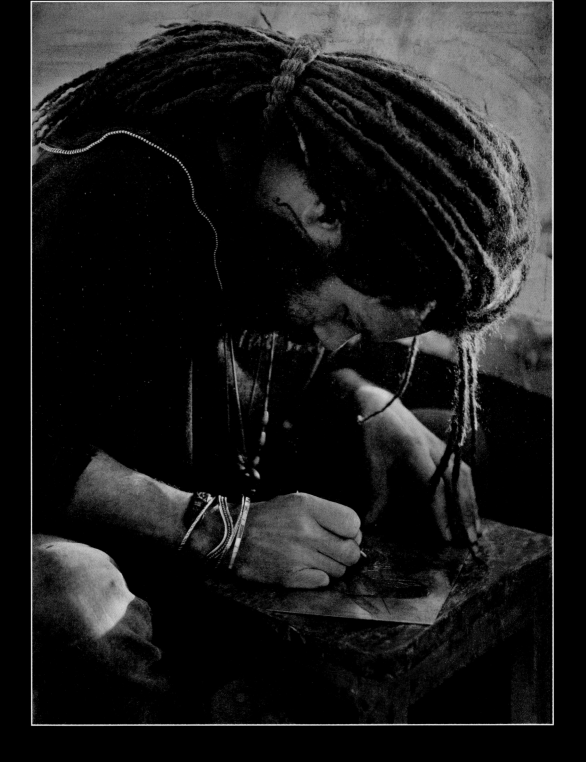

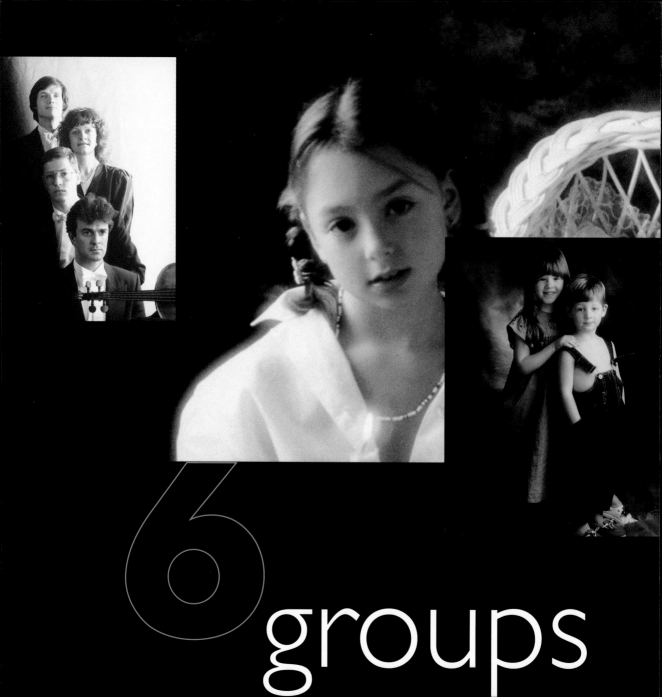

6 groups

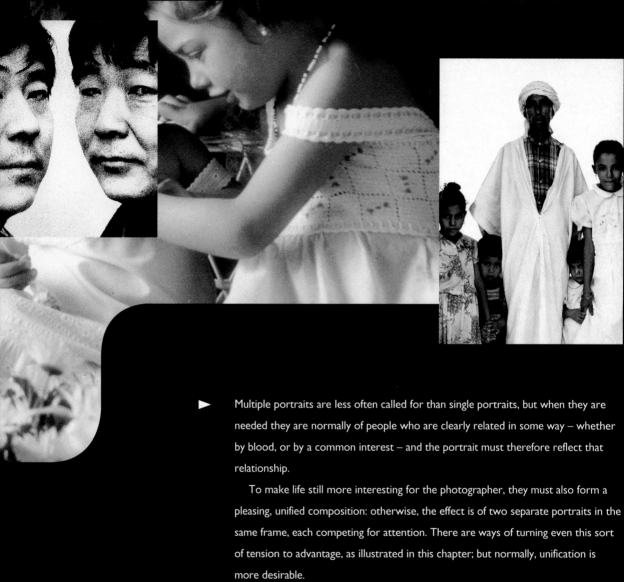

▶ Multiple portraits are less often called for than single portraits, but when they are needed they are normally of people who are clearly related in some way – whether by blood, or by a common interest – and the portrait must therefore reflect that relationship.

To make life still more interesting for the photographer, they must also form a pleasing, unified composition: otherwise, the effect is of two separate portraits in the same frame, each competing for attention. There are ways of turning even this sort of tension to advantage, as illustrated in this chapter; but normally, unification is more desirable.

The way to achieve this unification is generally by physical contact or at least by overlapping the characters. They may be ostensibly interested in one another – as with two children playing together – or they may each look at the camera, creating a commonalty of interest in that way. As a general rule, heads should be on different levels, even if that difference is fractional: two or more heads side by side, like coconuts in a fun-fair, will again look like two separate portraits in one frame. Different tilts of the heads, and some variation in body language, are also desirable.

Photographer: **Marc Joye**

Client: **James Ensor Quartet**

Use: **Editorial/poster**

Camera: **4x5in**

Lens: **150mm**

Film: **Kodak T-Max 100**

Exposure: **f/22**

Lighting: **Electronic flash: 2 heads**

Props and set: **16th-century violin**

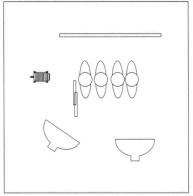

Plan View

► *Camera movements can be used to meet Scheimpflug conditions or to reduce depth of field selectively*

► *An advantage of 4x5in portraits is that the Polaroid tests are large enough to provide a useful guide to the final picture*

► *Monochrome portraits have a formal quality which can be useful as a device for establishing an air of gravity in the subjects*

J A M E S   E N S O R   Q U A R T E T

▼

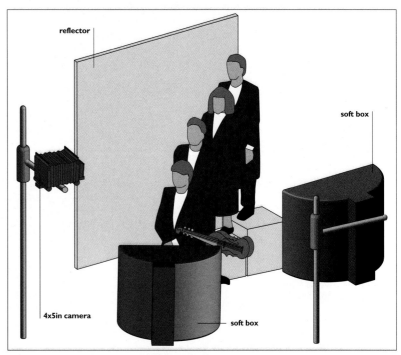

DEPTH OF FIELD IS RARELY A PROBLEM IN PORTRAITS, BUT HERE IT WAS. THE ONLY SOLUTION WAS TO USE CAMERA MOVEMENTS TO MEET THE SCHEIMPFLUG CONDITIONS IN ORDER TO HOLD ALL THE FACES IN FOCUS FROM FRONT TO BACK, ALONG WITH THE ANTIQUE VIOLIN.

Likewise, lighting in depth was required, and this was achieved with two soft boxes to camera right. The nearer one was about 1.5m (5ft) above the ground and was angled towards the violin (which was fixed to a stand) and the musicians. The more distant one was raised to about 2m (6½ft) to light the rising pose and was pretty much square on to the side of the group. The first musician was sitting on the ground; the second was standing; the third was on a small step; and the fourth was on a taller step. Fill came from a large reflector panel, 2x2m (6½x6½ft), to camera left.

Although 150mm is a "wide standard" lens on a 4x5in camera, it is ideal for group portraits: anything significantly longer than 180mm makes for uncomfortably long working distances.

Photographer's comment:

They liked the Polaroids and so we worked for four hours to make the smallest corrections in the expressions on their faces.

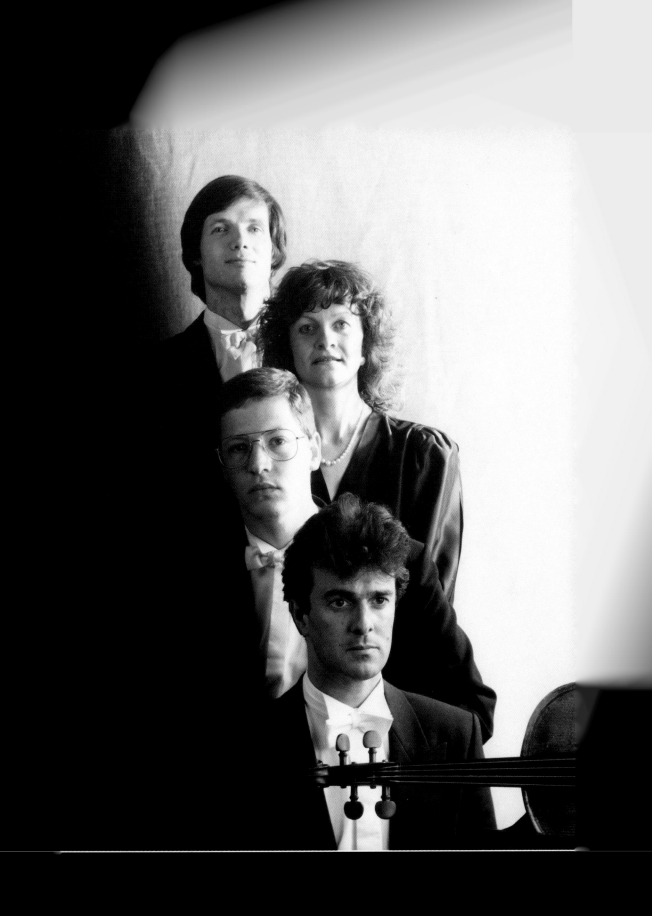

Photographer: **Dolors Porredon**

Client: **Studio**

Use: **Magazine**

Camera: **6x6cm**

Lens: **150mm**

Film: **Kodak Vericolor III**

Exposure: **f/8**

Lighting: **Electronic flash: 2 heads**

Props and set: **Painted backdrop**

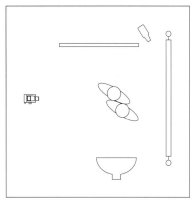

Plan View

► *Dark clothes absorb more light than pale ones – an obvious point, but easy to forget*

► *Position the subject with the darker clothes nearer the light*

► *Forget about political correctness if you want to please the children: little boys want to look masculine and little girls want to look feminine*

T W O   C H I L D R E N

▼

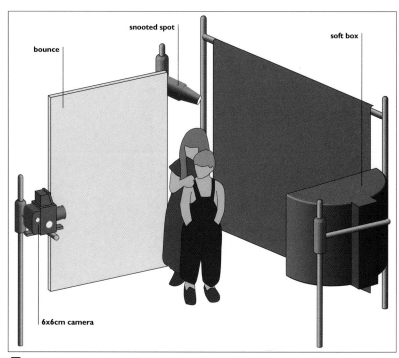

T HIS IS THE SORT OF PICTURE A THOUSAND PHOTOGRAPHERS COULD TAKE – INDEED, WHICH A THOUSAND ATTEMPT, EVERY DAY. WHY, THEN, ARE SO FEW PICTURES AS SUCCESSFUL AS THIS ONE? LIGHTING PLAYS A PART....

A 1x1m (40x40in) soft box to camera right is the key light. The shorter boy is positioned in front of the taller girl, as logic dictates. A bounce to camera left provides just the right amount of fill: because the light is soft, the shadows are not harsh in any case. The size and reflectivity of the bounce are important, though: it must be both large and quite highly reflective. The old standby of a

240x120cm (8x4ft) sheet of expanded polystyrene would work very well. A snooted spot to light the painted background completes the lighting plot.

As well as the light, the co-ordination of colour is important. Both children are in blue, but the darker colour is both more masculine (it matters, even at that age) and closer to the key light, where it is inevitably more strongly illuminated.

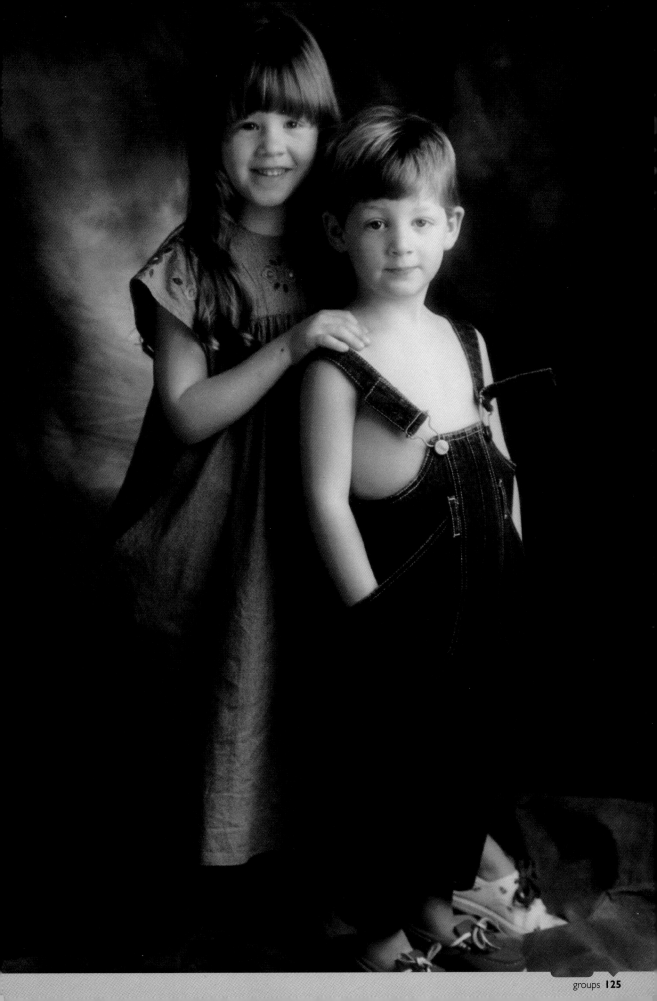

J U G A N D O

▼

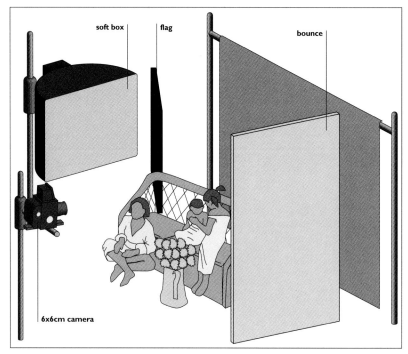

soft box | flag | bounce

6x6cm camera

Photographer: **Dolors Porredon**

Client: **Studio**

Use: **Poster**

Camera: **6x6cm**

Lens: **80mm**

Film: **Kodak Vericolor III**

Exposure: **f/8**

Lighting: **Electronic flash: 1 soft box**

Props and set: **Painted backdrop**

ANYONE WHO DECRIES THE FORMAL TRADITION IN PORTRAITS SHOULD EXAMINE THIS PICTURE CLOSELY. THE CHILDREN ARE HARDLY DRESSED TO PLAY, OR CAUGHT UNAWARES; BUT WHY SHOULD THEY BE? EVERYONE HAS SEVERAL SIDES TO HIS OR HER CHARACTER, AND THE CHARMING SEMI-FORMALITY OF THIS PHOTOGRAPH COULD HARDLY BE BETTERED.

The lighting is of the style commonly called "Rembrandt", with the principal subjects seemingly spotlit among generous shadows. The white clothing of the children is less reminiscent of Rembrandt, who worked principally with rich colours, but it emphasizes the purity and innocence of childhood. What is more, the folds of the children's clothes are beautifully delineated by the relatively small soft box (80x100cm/32x40in) to camera left, which is the sole light.

A black flag beside the soft box shades the background, which would otherwise be over-lit by spill, while a large white bounce to camera right provides the fill. The white clothes also act as a sort of "internal fill", bouncing light around to create a very airy mood against the dark, painted backdrop.

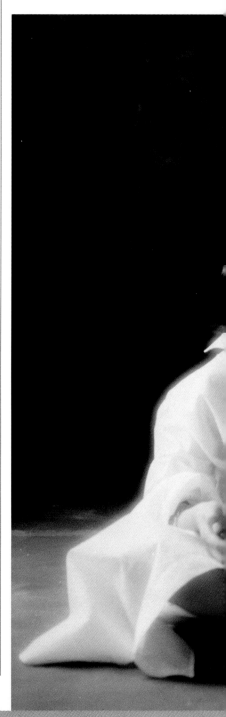

► Dark clothes or jeans may be more practical, but why should children always be dressed in practical clothes?

► White wickerwork should be an accessory to creative posing, not a substitute for it

► One little girl is showing her knickers; it may be better to adjust the dress a little to avoid this

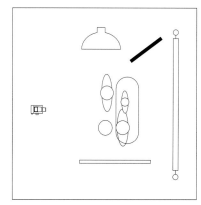

Plan View

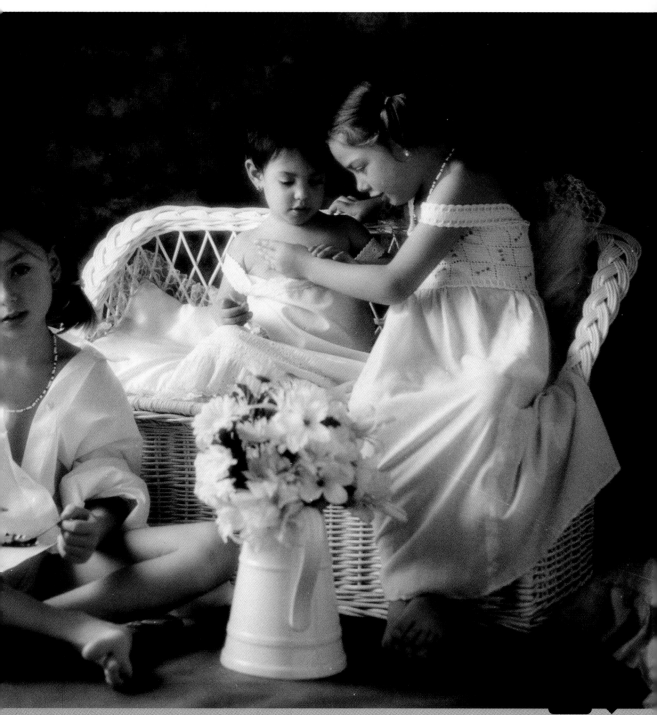

Photographer: **Frank Drake**

Client: **Peter Gabriel/Real World Records/
Virgin Records**

Use: **Record cover**

Subjects: **Guo Yue (left) Guo Yi (right)**

Assistant: **Sarah Ménage**

Art director: **E.A. Tredwell**

Camera: **35mm**

Lens: **35–135mm at 110mm**

Film: **Ilford FP4**

Exposure: **1/60 second at f/5.6**

Lighting: **Mixed: see text**

Props and set: **White background**

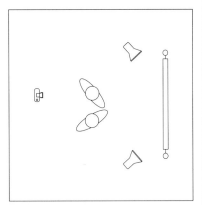

Plan View

► *Combine "reportage" (on-camera)
lighting with a separately lit background
for a dramatic effect*

► *Grain screens are often an easier
alternative than using fast films and
processing in paper developer for
maximum grain*

► *Remember the importance of catchlights
in eyes*

G U O   B R O T H E R S

▼

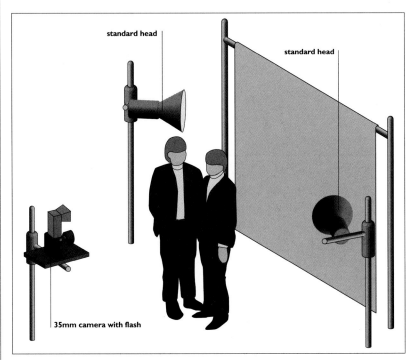

PRINTING AN FP4 NEGATIVE THROUGH A HEAVY GRAIN SCREEN PRESERVED THE TONALITY
AND CONTRAST OF FP4, AS COMPARED WITH THE TONALITY AND CONTRAST OF A FILM
DELIBERATELY "PUSHED" FOR GRAIN. THE LIGHTING IS, HOWEVER, DECEPTIVELY SIMPLE.

The background is lit with two tungsten
floods to give a slightly lighter tone than
the faces of the two brothers (this part
of the exposure is controlled by shutter
speed as well as aperture). The only
other lighting is an on-camera electronic
flash, where the exposure is of course
controlled solely by aperture.

This is a surprisingly sophisticated
technique. On-camera flash gives a
dramatic, "reportage" effect, which is
enhanced by the grain screen; but the
results do not look like on-camera flash
because the background is separately
illuminated to be lighter than the
brothers. The single catch-light in the
eyes is clear and effective, and there is
the kind of resolution reminiscent of ring
flash – though the use of a non-ring flash
also introduces a surprising degree of
modelling.

Photographer's comment:

*The brothers were barely speaking to one another, and I brought them as close together as I
could in order to exploit that tension. I think it worked.*

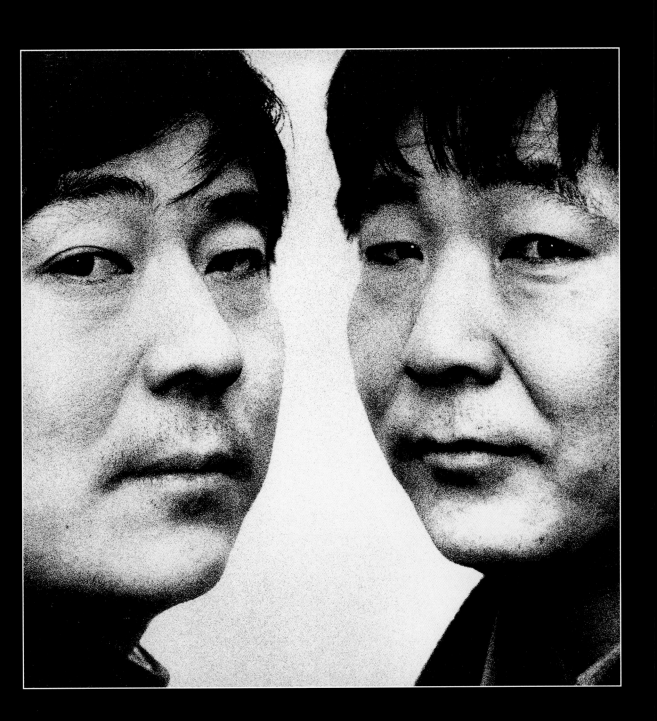

STRANGE TRINITY

▼

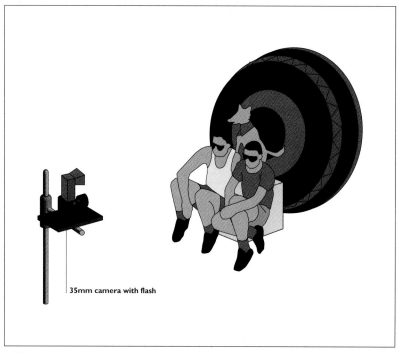

35mm camera with flash

"THIS SHOT BREAKS SEVERAL 'RULES' OF LIGHTING. IT WAS TAKEN AT NOON WITH THE SUN OVERHEAD, WITH FULL-FRONTAL ON-CAMERA FLASH TO ILLUMINATE THE UGLY SHADOWS CAST BY THE OVERHEAD SUN — AND THE CAMERA'S BUILT-IN FLASH CAST THE SHADOW OF THE LENS INTO THE PICTURE!"

Photographer: **Lewis Lang**

Use: **Exhibition/print sales**

Camera: **35mm**

Lens: **20mm**

Film: **Fujichrome 100 RDP**

Exposure: **Not recorded**

Lighting: **Daylight plus on-camera flash**

Props and Set: **Truck wheel**

As usual, Lewis sums up his own photography best. He goes on: "Normally, these 'three strikes' would justify throwing such a shot into the trash, but here they add up to a powerfully wild and wacky portrait — the lens's shadow over the bottom of the two gentlemen's faces makes them appear more ominous/sinister/mysterious, and the smiling dog seems to agree."

He also describes the light as "Weegee-esque", after the New York photographer who gained fame and notoriety for his harshly-lit scene-of-crime shots; an example of the intellectual resonances which often suffuse powerful pictures, whether we recognize their origins or not.

All too often, photographers ask other people what will "work" in a picture — and are too often willing to accept others' views. Lewis Lang demonstrates that the best answer is normally, "Try it!"

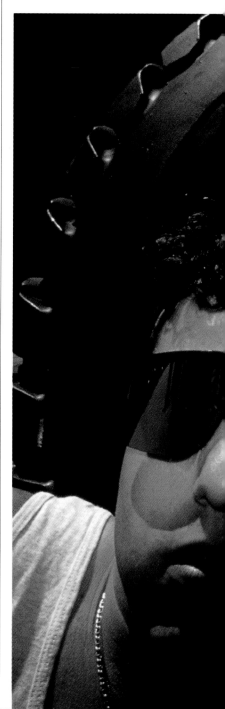

► On-camera flash can be exploited in a surprising variety of ways

► Harsh lighting, bright colours and simple shapes often go together well

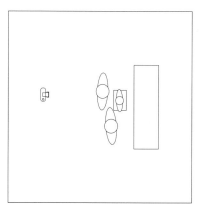

Plan View

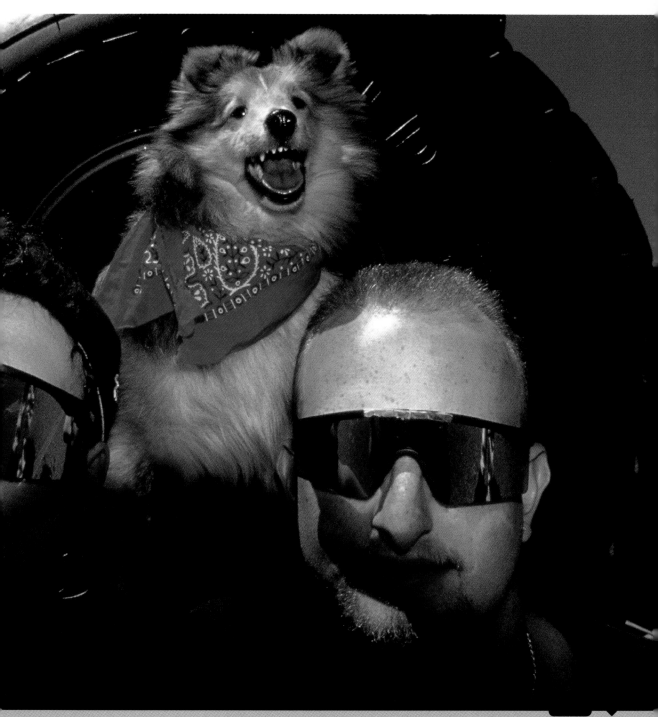

Photographer: **Alan Sheldon**

Client: *Elle* **magazine**

Use: **Editorial**

Assistant: **Nick Henry**

Camera: **6x7cm**

Lens: **165mm**

Film: **Agfa APX 25**

Exposure: **1/125 second at f/8**

Lighting: **Daylight: see text**

Props and set: **Built "lighting box": see text**

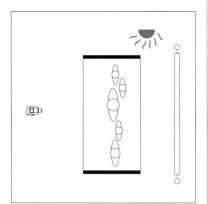

Plan View

A L G E R I A N   F A M I L Y

▼

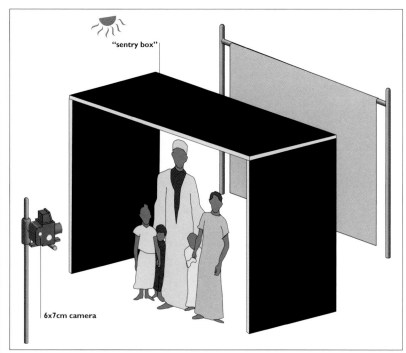

THIS WAS SHOT USING A DEVELOPMENT OF THE "SENTRY BOX" TECHNIQUE DESCRIBED ON PAGE 72. THE BACKGROUND IS 3×3M (10×10FT) WHILE THE BOX IS MADE FROM TWO 120×240CM (4×8FT) BLACK UPRIGHTS AND AN IMPROVISED ROOF.

The increased size of the custom-made backdrop of eyeletted canvas stretched over a collapsible frame means there is no problem with its edges intruding into the picture, even when it is placed well behind the box (as here) so that it is lit by bright sun while the subjects in the box are shaded by it. Because the backdrop is independently supported (it was in fact secured against the side of the photographer's van), both the backdrop and the box can be manoeuvred into the appropriate position with respect to the sun. The subjects come from Berber villages, North Africa.

► *A large background and a significantly longer than standard lens reduces problems with the edge of the background showing (165mm on 6x7cm is equivalent to 240–280mm on 4x5in)*

► *Bright sun on the background and shaded sun on the foreground gives a naturally high key effect*

Photographer's comment:

I had to improvise a roof because I could not get them all under the standard 1.2m (4ft) wide roof.

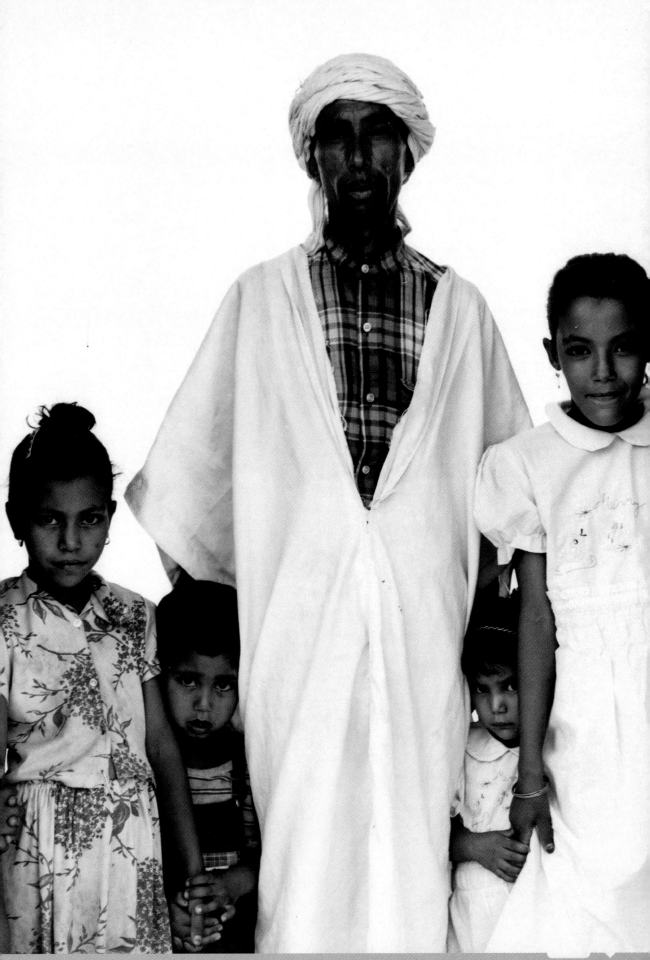

Photographer: **Frank P. Wartenberg**

Use: **Portfolio**

Camera: **35mm**

Lens: **105mm**

Film: **Polaroid Polagraph**

Exposure: **Not recorded; probably f/4 to f/5.6**

Lighting: **Electronic flash: 4 heads**

Props and set: **Grey background paper**

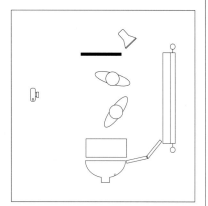

Plan View

▼

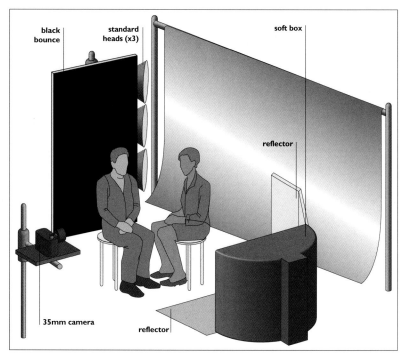

A SINGLE LARGE SOFT BOX TO CAMERA RIGHT IS THE KEY AND ONLY LIGHT HERE; IT IS FURTHER SOFTENED BY A LARGE SILVER REFLECTOR ON THE FLOOR IN FRONT OF IT, AND ANOTHER LARGE SILVER REFLECTOR BESIDE IT.

A black bounce to camera left means that there is no fill, and the choice of a contrasty film (Polaroid Polagraph) further accentuates contrast: the dark parts of the faces merge into the black background. This technique, using the kind of skin reflections which for want of a better term are often called "specular", is feasible with monochrome but with colour can lead to an unpleasantly greasy or sweaty looking skin texture.

With such contrasty lighting, a large part of the skill in the picture comes from very precise posing, so that the bright part of the face to camera left overlaps with the deeply shadowed part of the face to camera right.

► *"Specular" skin reflections often work better in monochrome than in colour*

► *Abrupt transitions from light to dark require careful composition if the picture is not to appear "busy"*

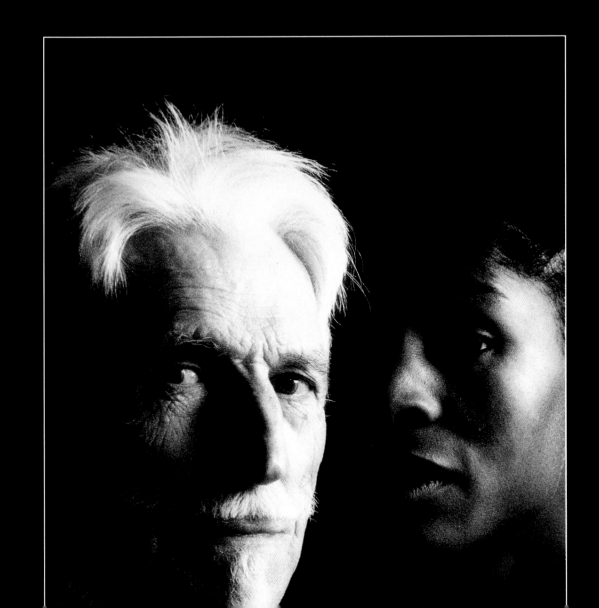

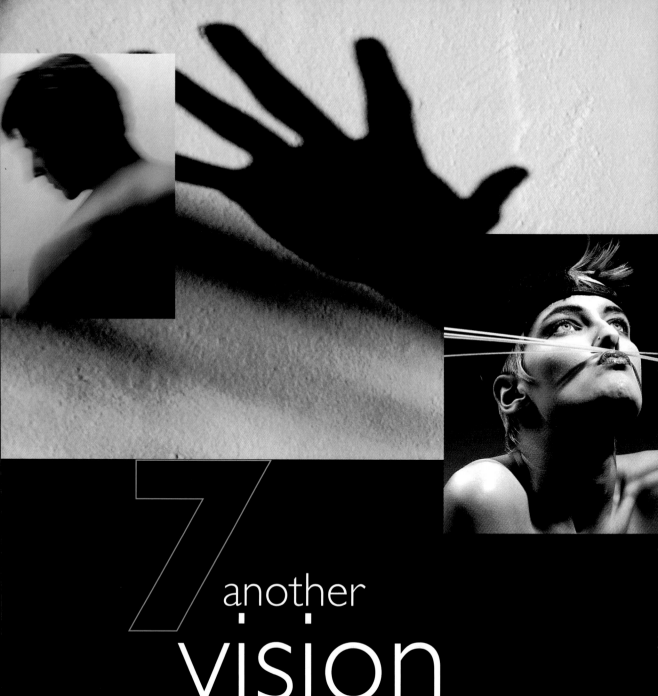

another
vision

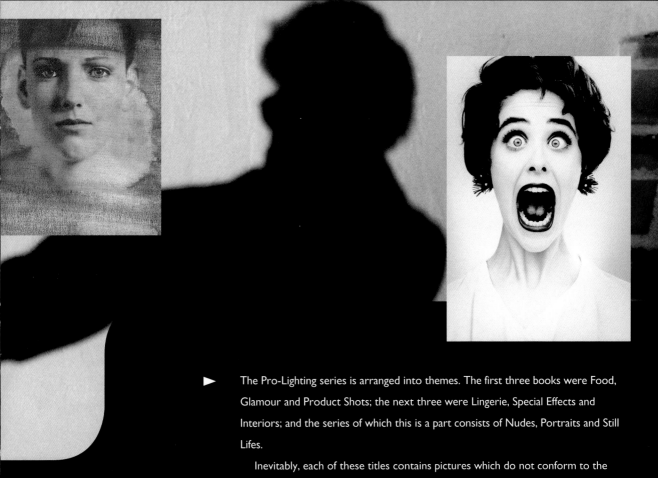

The Pro-Lighting series is arranged into themes. The first three books were Food, Glamour and Product Shots; the next three were Lingerie, Special Effects and Interiors; and the series of which this is a part consists of Nudes, Portraits and Still Lifes.

Inevitably, each of these titles contains pictures which do not conform to the conventional definition of the theme chosen, but which equally fall within the ambit of the book. Here, as in other books in the series, they are gathered in the last chapter. There are shadows and special effects, and unusual techniques and humour, and pictures which are just … different.

If they have a unifying theme or message, it is this: the portrait photographer explores both the nature of the subject and his or her own nature; though this is true of many of the pictures in other chapters, too. Perhaps more importantly, while the portraits in this chapter may seem to varying degrees to be "way out", they may yet suggest other ways of seeing which will become familiar in a decade's or a century's time. Compare a 1940s Hollywood portrait with a 19th century Victorian portrait and a 1960s "Swinging London" portrait, and it becomes clear that each generation has its own way of seeing. One of the most fascinating things about this book has been seeing how different photographers interpret their generation's world-picture. Portraiture has not ceased to evolve; nor will it.

▼

Photographer: **Rudi Mühlbauer**

Use: **Self-promotion**

Model: **Eva**

Camera: **6x6cm**

Lens: **80mm**

Film: **Agfa Pan ISO 100/21**

Exposure: **1 second at f/2.8**

Lighting: **Tungsten**

Props and set: **White background, black leather jacket**

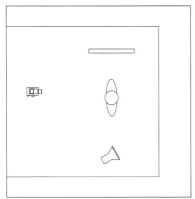

Plan View

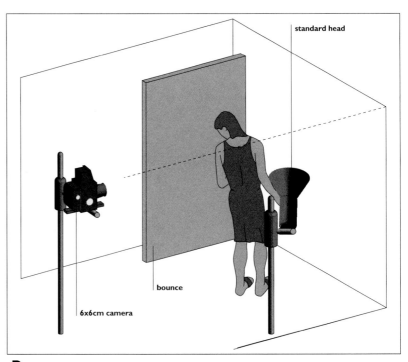

standard head

bounce

6x6cm camera

P EOPLE USED TO CALL A PORTRAIT A "LIKENESS", AND COMMONLY DEMANDED JUST THAT: A PICTURE WHICH WAS AS LITERAL AS A POLICE MUG-SHOT, BUT PREFERABLY MORE FLATTERING. TODAY, WE ARE PERHAPS MORE OPEN TO ARTISTIC INTERPRETATION.

Rudi Mühlbauer used a low, white ceiling (3.2m/10½ft) to diffuse the light: the 1000 Watt lamp was mounted on a lighting stand roughly at head height (1.7m/5½ft) and bounced upwards. The subject was only 50cm (18in) from the wall, which served as a background and was lit solely with spill from the key. A white bounce to camera left and just out of shot, provided some fill on the face.

Asking the subject to move during the exposure is necessarily experimental, and it is normally necessary to shoot a good number of exposures from which only a few – or even just one – may be usable. Finally, the monochrome negative was printed on Kodak Ektacolor Ultra paper in order to achieve the colour.

► *Deliberate subject movement during exposure is normally most effective in the 1 second to 1/8 second range*

► *Printing monochrome negatives onto colour paper gives a wide range of colour options*

► *Second-curtain flash synch (or synch on the closing of a leaf shutter) can be very effective, though it was not used here*

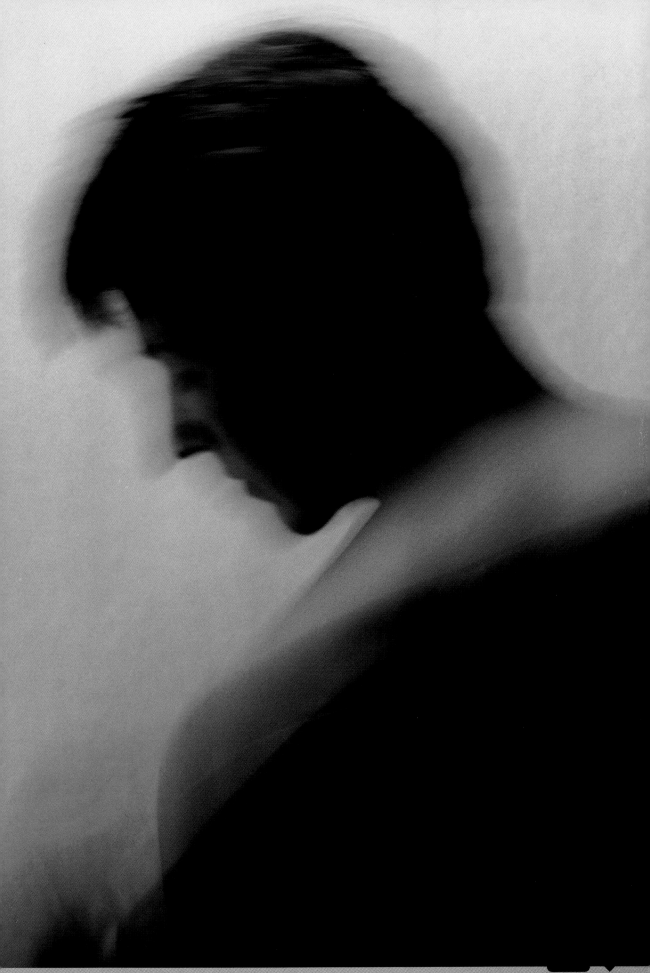

DARK ANGEL

▼

Photographer: **Lewis Lang**

Use: **Exhibition/Print Sales**

Subject: **Lewis Lang**

Camera: **35mm**

Lens: **25–50mm zoom at 25mm**

Film: **Fujichrome 100 RDP**

Exposure: **About 1/125 at f/16**

Lighting: **Direct setting sun**

Props and set: **Sta. Barbara County Court House, California**

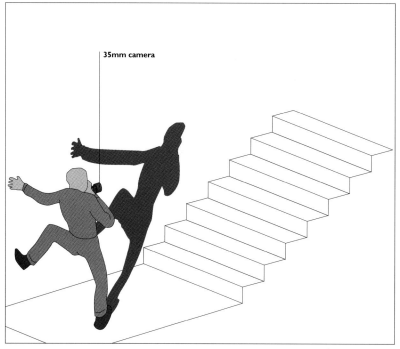

35mm camera

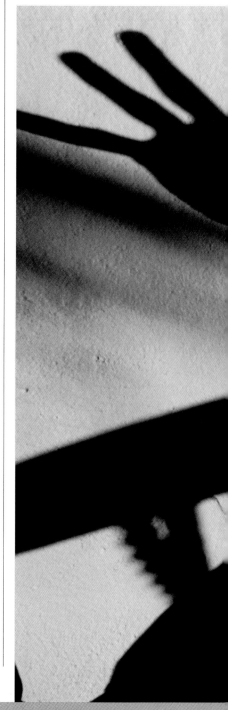

Remarkably, this is a self-portrait. The shadow of the camera is blocked by the shadow of the head; it is pointed at the wall, and slightly to the right, at an angle of 45° or less.

Most photographers are intrigued by the light of the setting sun, and want to play with it – but to get the best results you have to plan ahead, so as to be in the right place at the right time, and you have to hope there is no cloud. Californians, more than most people, can generally rely on the latter.

Much the same considerations apply to shadows: they are fascinating to play with, but getting a successful shadow picture depends on very precise exposure (usually slightly under, against a white background, in order to get adequate density) as well as a combination of imagination and determination.

Although Lewis works with formats other than 35mm, he believes that the very best 35mm equipment and materials can deliver more than adequate quality even for fine art photography – but they must be the very best.

Photographer's comment:

A low, west-coast setting sun at an oblique angle to the court house, and some deft positioning of my body, enabled me to get a shadow that is both a flat shape and appears to recede three-dimensionally.

- ► Plan ahead to be in the right place at sunset

- ► Look for a white-painted or at least pale-coloured wall

- ► Use stairs, etc, to create distortions in the shadows

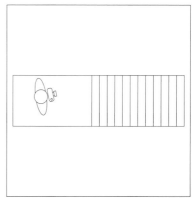

Plan View

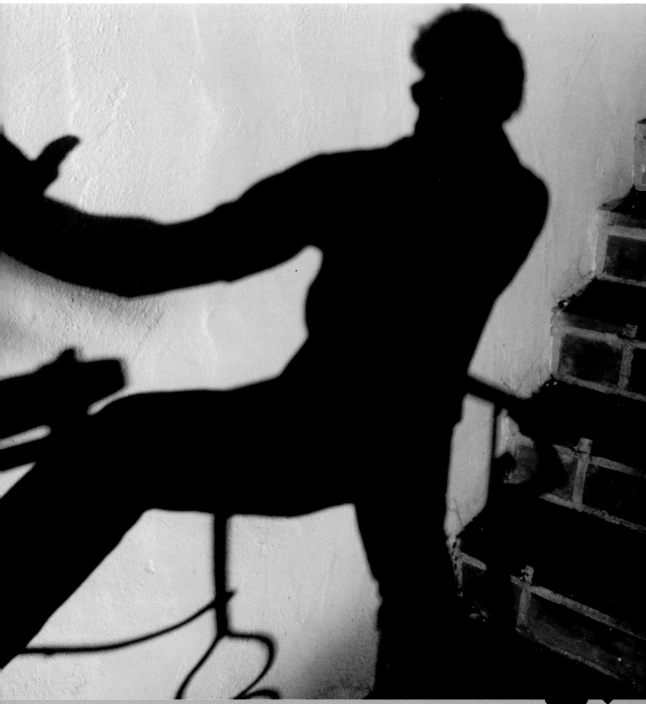

Photographer: **Kay Hurst, K Studios**

Use: **Exhibition**

Model: **Carron Bradley**

Assistant: **Katy Niker**

Camera: **4x5in**

Lens: **360mm**

Film: **Polaroid Type 55 rated at EI 25**

Exposure: **f/11**

Lighting: **Electronic flash: single soft box**

Props and set: **Lastolite painted background**

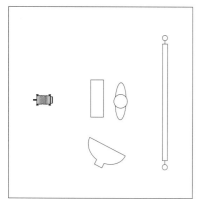

Plan View

F A C E / C L O U D

▼

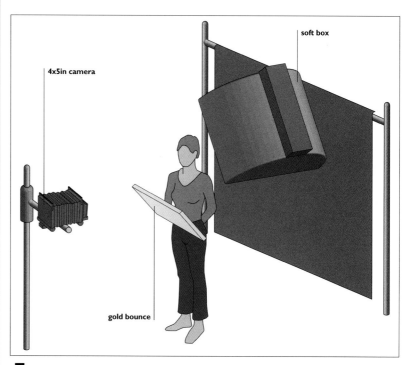

THE LIGHTING HERE IS VERY SIMPLE INDEED: NO MORE THAN A SINGLE SOFT BOX TO CAMERA RIGHT AND SOMEWHAT ABOVE EYE LEVEL, SUPPLEMENTED BY A GOLD BOUNCE UNDER THE MODEL'S FACE TO LIGHTEN THE SHADOWS UNDER THE NOSE AND CHIN.

The monochrome print (on Kentmere Art Classic) was toned sepia, then reworked with a fairly dry gouache using a number of painting techniques which K has developed: for instance, applying colour with a heavy, stiff stencil brush, then removing it again with a soft Japanese brush. The removal of paint, with a soft-edged effect reminiscent of clouds or watermarks, is as important as the application. As with many of K's pictures, both the simplicity of the lighting and the complexity of the afterwork are deceptive. Look "through" the afterwork and there is a very direct, strong portrait: look at the afterwork, and it is very much a complement to the portrait, rather than a gratuitous overlay.

► *Afterwork requires a strong portrait to begin with: one can rarely "save" a poor picture by painting over it*

► *Pictures for exhibition often demonstrate subtler tones than those for reproduction, where these subtleties may be lost*

► *Originality of vision is often the result of both experiment and a mastery of more conventional techniques*

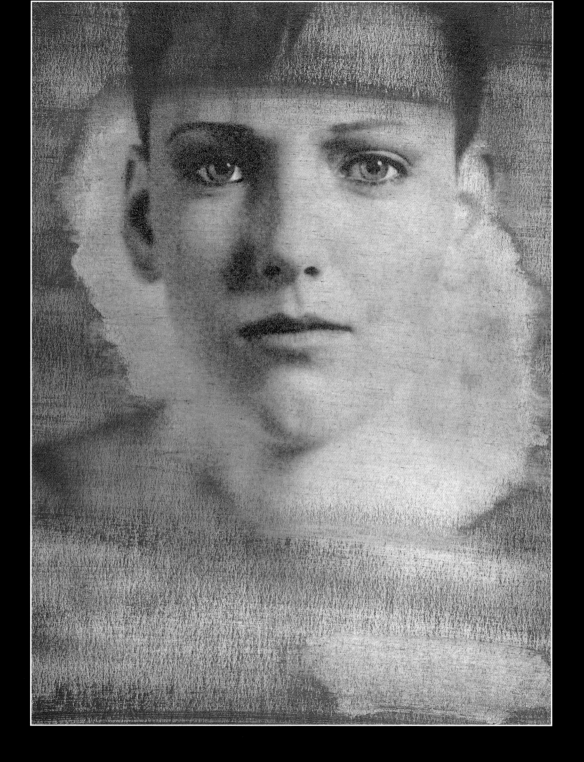

Z E N A

▼

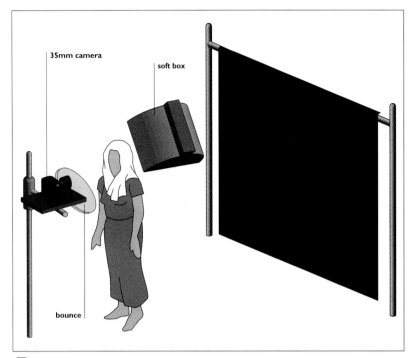

Photographer: **David Dray**

Use: **Stock/library**

Model: **Zena Christenson**

Camera: **35mm**

Lens: **100mm**

Film: **Fujicolor ISO 100 (negative)**

Exposure: **f/8**

Lighting: **Electronic flash: 1 head**

Props and set: **White paper, length of muslin material**

Labels in diagram: 35mm camera, soft box, bounce

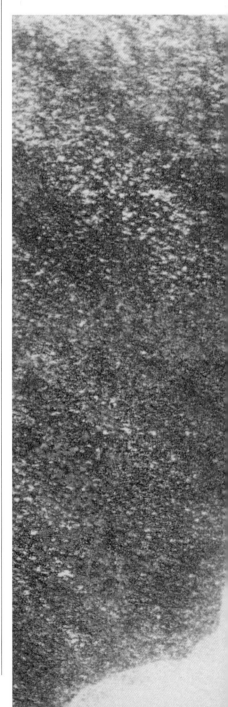

THIS PICTURE DEMONSTRATES A TECHNIQUE FOR WHICH DAVID IS NOTED, THAT OF COLOUR PHOTOCOPY TRANSFER. THE ORIGINAL PHOTOGRAPH IS MADE INTO A COLOUR PHOTOCOPY, THEN TRANSFERRED BY A SOLVENT TECHNIQUE ONTO WATER-COLOUR PAPER WHICH GIVES A UNIQUE EFFECT.

The subject is well in front of the background, which is about 2.5m (8ft) behind her; the amount of spill reaching it is therefore trivial. The only light is a small 40x40cm (16x16in) soft box set rather above the model's eye-line and angled down at her: it is about 1m (40in) from her. Immediately out of shot, low and to camera left, is a bounce which throws light back up into the model's face. The white muslin also acts as a combination flag (or at least scrim) and bounce, partially shading the model's face but also reflecting light down onto the bounce.

► When pictures are subject to after-treatment of this kind, there is rarely any need to use formats larger than 35mm

► A landscape (horizontal) composition emphasizes the drape of the muslin head-covering; a conventional portrait (vertical) orientation would have created a completely different mood

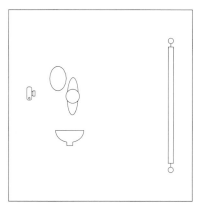

Plan View

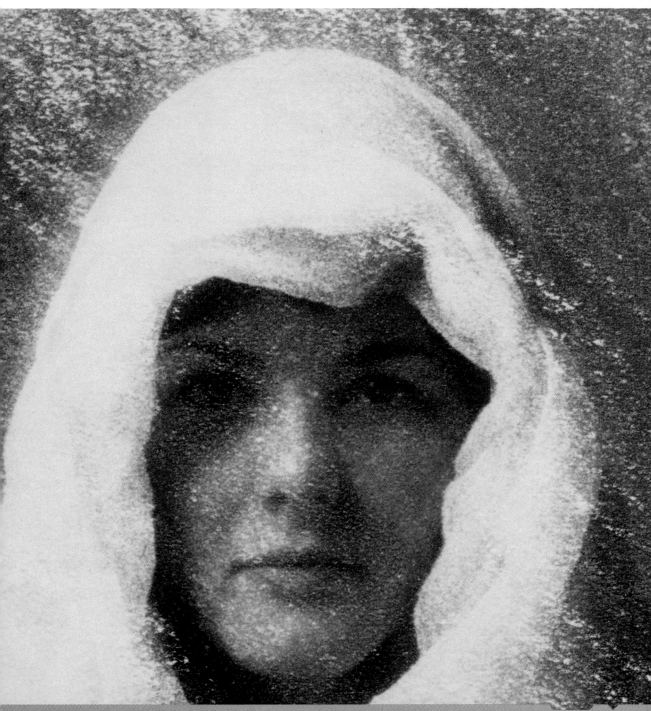

PORTRAIT OF SIMONE

▼

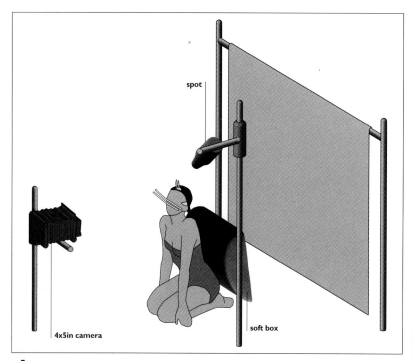

spot

4x5in camera

soft box

Photographer: **Peter Laqua**

Use: **Competition entry**

Model: **Simone**

Stylist: **Silke Schöepfer**

Camera: **4x5in**

Lens: **300mm**

Film: **Monochrome transparency**

Exposure: **Not recorded**

Lighting: **Electronic flash: 2 heads**

Props and set: **Spaghetti**

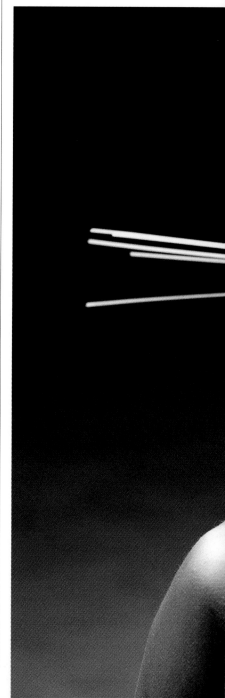

ALL CHILDREN MAKE "MOUSTACHES" BY HOLDING SOMETHING BETWEEN THEIR TOP LIP AND THEIR NOSES — BUT MOST PEOPLE STOP WHEN THEY ARE CHILDREN AND DO NOT TAKE IT TO EXTREMES LIKE THIS! THE REVERSED BASEBALL CAP ADDS TO THE PLAYFUL SPIRIT.

The key and indeed only light on the face is a focusing spotlight, high and to camera right, shining more or less straight down on the model: look at the shadows in her ears. It has to be a focusing spot, as a snooted spot or honeycomb spot would not provide such directional light. A 70x130cm (28x50in) soft box behind and below the model illuminates the background, grading from light to dark; the texture of the background, normally invisible when it is lit frontally, adds to the composition.

► *Agfa's Scala direct-reversal film is available in 35mm, 120 and 4x5in; the only other convenient direct-reversal monochrome films come from Polaroid*

► *The exquisite detail of the 4x5in image should be visible, even in reproduction*

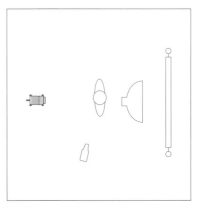

Plan View

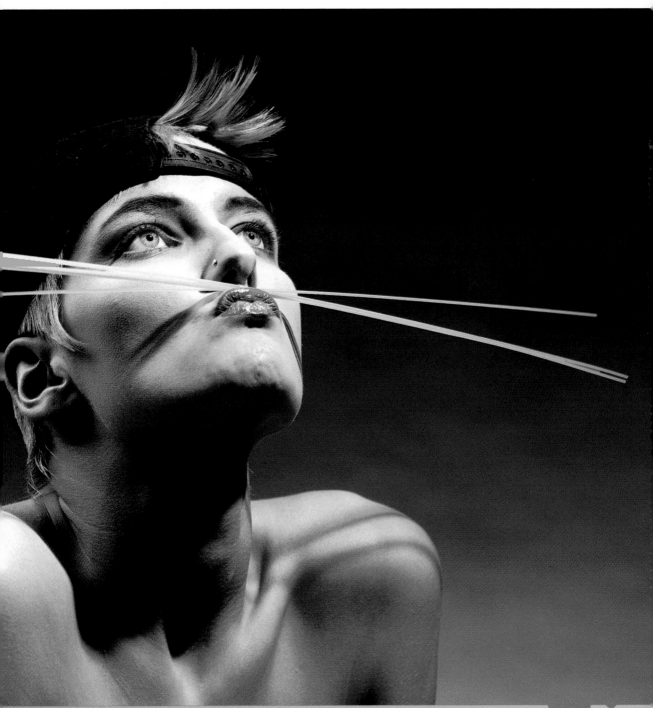

Photographer: **Benny De Grove**

Use: **Exhibition**

Camera operator: **Jan Hindzo**

Camera: **50x60cm (20x24in)**

Lens: **Not recorded**

Film: **Polaroid 50x60cm**

Exposure: **Not recorded (double exposure)**

Lighting: **Electronic flash: double exposure
(see text)**

Props and set: **Wall (see text)**

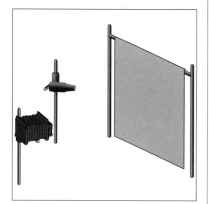

First Exposure

► *Polaroid's monster camera in Prague
gives results unlike any other*

► *Lighting for rough textures and lighting
for skin are quite different*

► *Flags and scrims may be necessary to
control local areas in a double exposure*

THE GIRL FROM PRAHA

▼

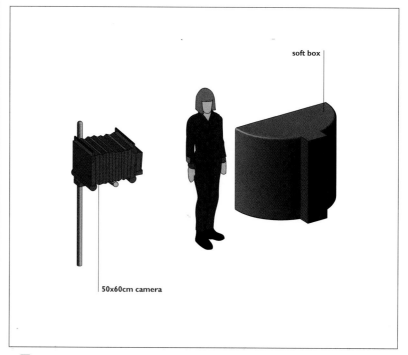

soft box

50x60cm camera

THE TITLE OF THE PICTURE GIVES THE FIRST CLUE; THE FORMAT OF THE CAMERA GIVES THE SECOND. BENNY DE GROVE IS AMONG THE FEW WHO HAVE BEEN PRIVILEGED TO USE THE GREAT CAMERA OF PRAGUE, ONE OF THE POLAROID 20x24IN MODELS.

The first exposure, of the collaged wall, was lit with a spot from camera left to give maximum texture. The wall is made of many materials: leather, sacking and building materials.

The second exposure, of the girl, was lit with an 80cm (30in) square soft box from camera right, almost at right angles to the first exposure. This is in absolute defiance of the normal rule concerning double exposures, but in the specialized circumstances it is essential: the girl is at once part of the structure, and of a higher order of creation.

Photographer's comment:

In order to give the impression that the girl is part of the structure, some parts had to be underexposed.

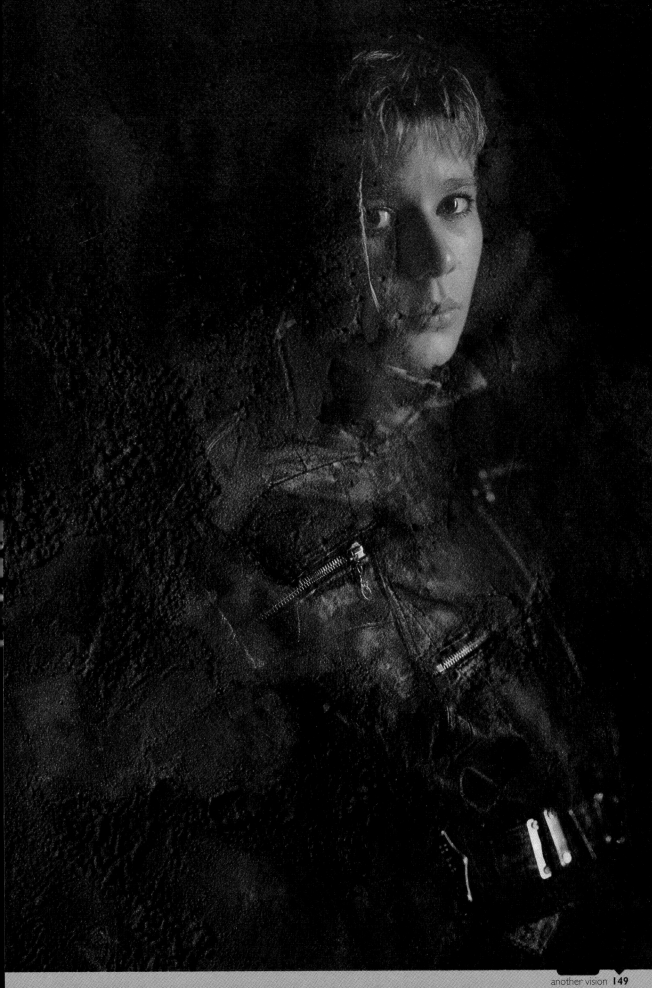

Photographer: **Peter Barry**

Use: **Christmas card**

Model: **Peter Barry**

Make-up and hair: **Celia Hunter**

Camera: **6x6cm**

Lens: **150mm**

Film: **Ilford FP4**

Exposure: **f/11**

Lighting: **Electronic flash: 2 heads**

Props and set: **Scissors, paper cut-out**

Christmas trees

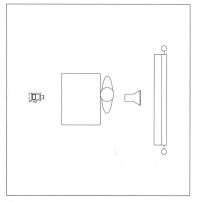

Plan View

► *Classic "horror" lighting is from underneath, but flat frontal light can be just as menacing*

► *There is a place for humour in photography, though successful humour is not always easy to achieve*

PETER SCISSORHANDS

▼

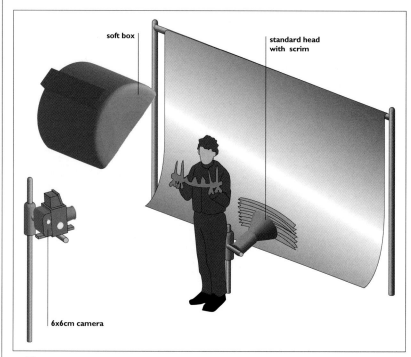

soft box

standard head
with scrim

6x6cm camera

PETER BARRY'S CHRISTMAS CARDS ARE EAGERLY AWAITED BY HIS FRIENDS AND BUSINESS CONTACTS EVERY YEAR: HE HAS BEEN THE JOKER FROM *BATMAN*, A PANTOMIME DAME, SCROOGE, THE MASK AND MORE. THE LIGHTING ON THIS IS ACTUALLY ONE OF THE SIMPLER ONES.

A single soft box, 150cm (5ft) square, was placed directly over the camera for a dead flat "horror film" light; reflections off the blades of the scissors (which were taped to his hands) were essential, as was the threatening leather jacket which also reflected the light well. A large print was made, and the cut-out Christmas trees were hand-coloured (they were white in the original).

The painted canvas background was lit by a single diffused light on the floor behind the subject: a scrim over a standard head.

A great deal obviously depends on the make-up, and on the topicality of the image: this was made in the year that *Edward Scissorhands* was released.

Photographer's comment:

I do this sort of thing every year. It's fun, and it is effective promotion as well.

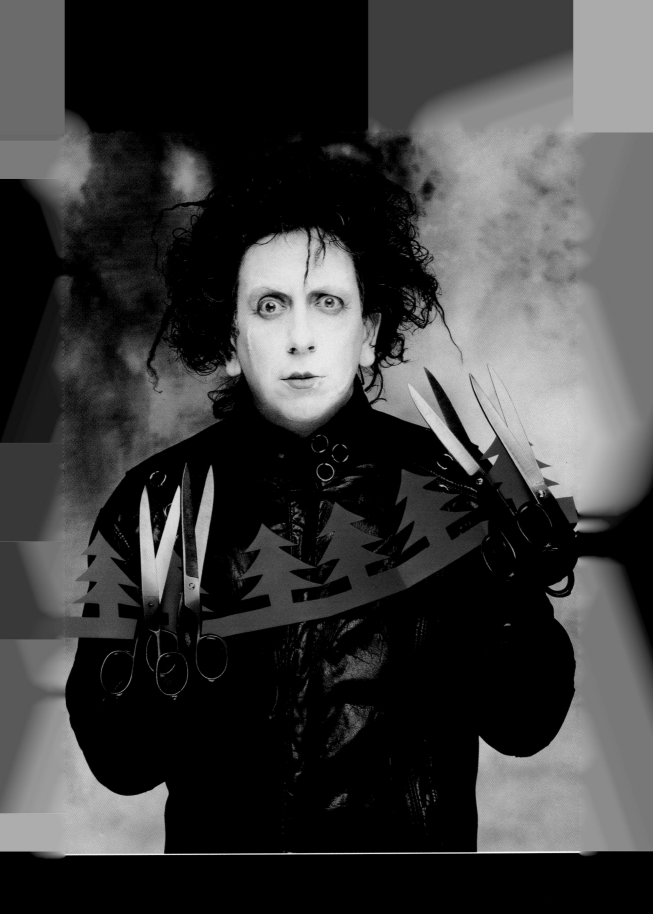

another

Photographer: **Johnny Boylan**

Client: **Terence Higgins Trust**

Use: **Publicity (not used)**

Assistant: **Christine Donnier-Valentine**

Camera: **6x7cm**

Lens: **180mm**

Film: **Agfa APX 100 printed on lith paper**

Exposure: **f/11**

Lighting: **Electronic flash: 4 heads**

Props and set: **White background**

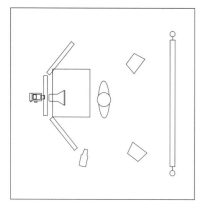

Plan View

▼

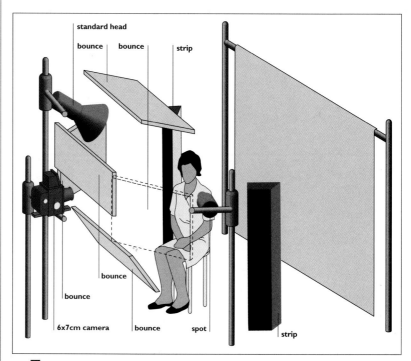

standard head

bounce   bounce   strip

bounce

bounce

6x7cm camera   bounce   spot

bounce

strip

THIS WAS FROM A SERIES OF PICTURES DESIGNED TO CONVEY EMOTION; IN THIS CASE, "HYSTERIA". RATHER THAN GOING FOR THE SORT OF HARSHLY-LIT PSEUDO-REPORTAGE SHOT WHICH SOME MIGHT CHOOSE, JOHNNY BOYLAN WENT FOR A VERY FORMAL, GRAPHIC INTERPRETATION.

Two lights were used on the subject, a hard top light from above (look at the shadows on the tongue) and a "beauty light" from the right, a soft spot which gives extra modelling: look at the differences between the two sides of the neck, and the cheeks.

The directional effects of these two lights are, however, much diminished by generous use of white expanded polystyrene bounces all around the subject; you have to look closely to see that the light is directional at all, though the modelling of the face would have been far less obvious if it were not.

Finally, the high-key background comes from two strip-lights on either side of the subject; it is lit about half a stop down from the main subject.

► *Directional lighting, no matter how heavily modified with reflectors, always gives more modelling than flat frontal lighting*

► *The reflections on the hair are from the bright background*

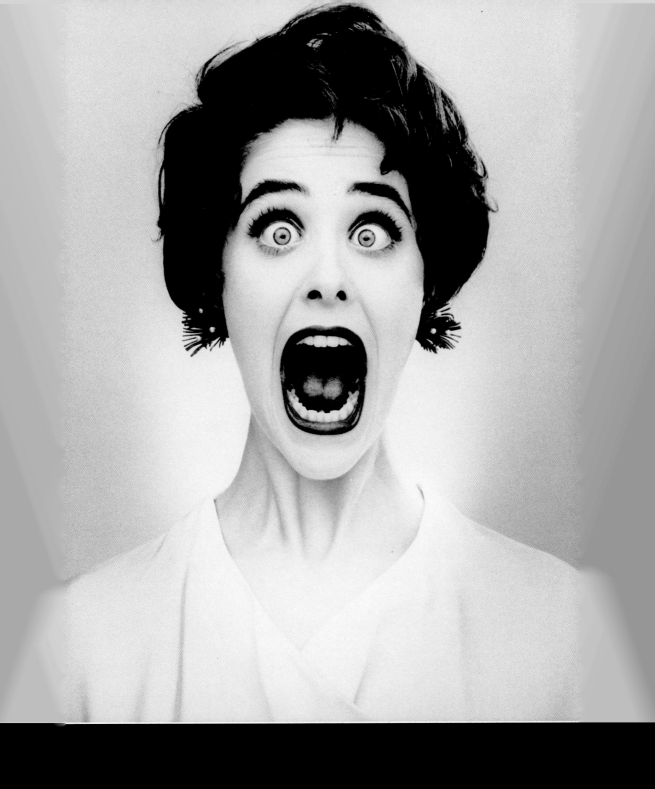

another

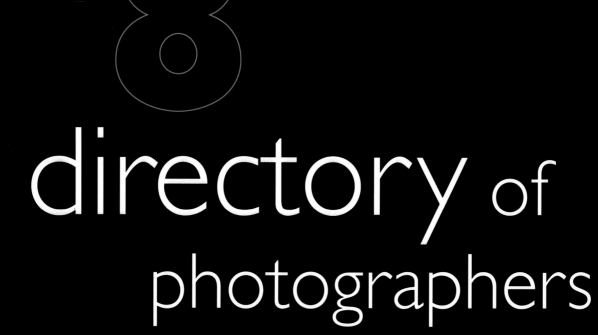

8

directory of
photographers

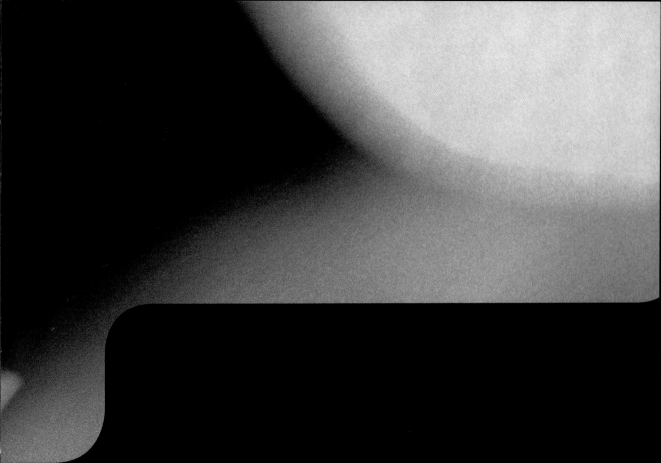

Photographer: **JOHNNY BOYLAN**
Address: THE SOAP FACTORY, 9 PARK HILL
LONDON SW4 9NS
Telephone: + 44 (0) 171 622 1214
Mobile: + 44 (0) 831
Fax: + 44 (0) 171 498 6445
Biography: *Photography becomes a way of life, an obsession. Luckily for me it also provides a good living. Every new commission, whatever it is, is a challenge. That challenge need not necessarily be photographic. The sourcing of a location; a model; finding an unusual artefact; getting over the logistical problems of travelling to some backwater in another continent. Photography can be make-believe and fantasy, but most of all it is an art form of supplying your client. There is no room for error and there is no forgiving in supplying something that is unusable, whatever the reason. Enjoy!*
Portraits: pp 61, 101, 117, 153

Photographer: **PETER BARRY**
Studio: 57 FARRINGDON ROAD
LONDON EC4M 3JB
ENGLAND
Telephone: + 44 (0) 171 430 0966
Fax: + 44 (0) 171 430 0903
Biography: *Peter Barry's work is extremely varied – fashion, advertising, girls, still life and food – so every day is different, exciting and stimulating. Constantly learning and experimenting with new techniques, his two main passions are people and food. He has travelled all over the world and met many fascinating people and as a result he feels that photography is not so much work as a way of life.*
Portrait: p 151

Photographer: **MARIA CRISTINA CASSINELLI**
Address: VENEZUELA 1421
(1095) BUENOS AIRES
ARGENTINA
Telephone: + 58 (0) 541 381 8805
Fax: + 58 (0) 541 383 9323
Agent
(New York): BLACK STAR

116 EAST 27TH STREET
NEW YORK
NY 10016
Fax: +1 (0) 212 8890 2052
Biography: *Endowed with a unique creative style, Cristina represents with a clear identity and without spoiling the essence of the subjects, a still life, a portrait or an architectural oeuvre immersed in a landscape. One can recognize a directing thread, magical, in its diversity: innate sensitivity and a mature technique to combine in an image, aesthetics, light, design and subtle details …*
Portraits: pp 77, 78–79

Photographer: **BENNY DE GROVE**
Studio: FOTOSTUDIO DE GROVE
ZWIJNAARDSE STEENWEG 28A
9820 MERELBEKE
BELGIUM
Telephone: + 32 (0) 9 231 96 16
Fax: + 32 (0) 9 231 95 94
Biography: *Born 1957, I have been a photographer since 1984. Most of the time I work in publicity and illustration for magazines. For some time now I have been fascinated by triptychs. I like to make my pictures somehow symbolic: they must be a starting point for discussion, for thinking about.*
Portrait: p 149

Photographer: **FRANK DRAKE**
Studio: PELICAN STUDIOS
17 GOLDNEY ROAD
CLIFTON
BRISTOL BS8 4RB
ENGLAND
Telephone/Fax:+ 44 (0) 117 92 62 557
Biography: *Self taught; decided on photography as a fine art after meeting Cartier-Bresson in Paris in the early 70s. Worked with Peter Gabriel's Real World Records for 6 years, photographing musicians from around the world. Starting now (1996) on fashion photography after studying Art and Social Context at University of West of England.*
Portrait: p 129

Photographer: **DAVID DRAY**
Address: 60 MILTON AVENUE
MARGATE
KENT CT9 1TT
ENGLAND
Telephone: + 44 (0) 1843 22 36 40
Biography: *I am a graphic artist working on the Isle of Thanet, Kent, England. I trained at the Canterbury College of Art, where I first started using cellulose thinners to produce montages from gravure printing. Later I applied the thinners technique to colour photocopies to achieve results as illustrated. I use this technique with my own photography or (as appropriate) with other photographers' work to maintain complete control in design briefs.*
Portrait: pp 144–145

Photographer: **COLIN GLANFIELD**
Studio: PLOUGH STUDIOS
9 PARK HILL
LONDON SW4 9NS
ENGLAND
Telephone: + 44 (0) 171 622 1939
Fax: + 44 (0) 171 627 5169
Biography: *Affectionately known to ex-assistants, clients and friends as "Uncle Colin", he has worked in virtually every branch of the profession – from travel to automobiles, from medical photography to advertising – for several decades without ever losing enthusiasm. As well as writing books and magazine articles on photographic subjects, he owns with his wife Jenny a large London hire studio in London's Park Hill "Photography Village": with other photographers and a pro lab next door. The photograph in this book comes from an ongoing project to document people with "lived-in" faces, using an 8x10 inch camera. As he says, "This should keep me going until I fall off my tripod."*
Portrait: p 51

Photographer: **PETER GOODRUM**
Address: 2 HILLEND COTTAGES
KEWSTOKE ROAD
WORLE
WESTON-SUPER-MARE
AVON BS22 9JY
ENGLAND
Telephone: + 44 (0) 1934 516 178
Biography: *Peter Goodrum has turned his hobby of the early 1980s into a career for the*

1990s and beyond. As a book illustrator, he was hit hard by the recession: clients, art directors and advertising agencies vanished overnight, so in 1993 he decided to do a degree in photography at Cheltenham. He now looks upon this as the best thing ever to happen to him, both for exploring new ideas and techniques and for his personal development. He now specializes in photographing people – he particularly likes to photograph artists – and works for editorial, advertising and corporate clients as well as establishing a growing reputation as a photographic printer.

Portrait: p 119

Photographer: **ROGER HICKS**
Address: ROGER & FRANCES
5 ALFRED ROAD
BIRCHINGTON
KENT CT7 9ND
ENGLAND
Telephone: + 44 (0) 1843 848 664
Fax: + 44 (0) 1843 848 665
Biography: *Roger is a wordsmith and photographer, both self-taught. He is the author of more than 50 books, including this one, as well as being a regular contributor to* The British Journal of Photography, Shutterbug, Darkroom User *and other photographic magazines. He has illustrated "How-To" books, historical/travel books and of course photography books, and has written on a wide variety of subjects: airbrushing, automotive subjects, the Tibetan cause and the American Civil War. He works with his American-born wife Frances E. Schultz on both self-originated and commissioned projects, to provide packages of words and pictures suitable for both sides of the Atlantic.*

Portrait: p 47

Photographer: **KAY HURST**
Studio: K STUDIOS
9 HAMPTON ROAD
GREAT LEVER
BOLTON
LANCASHIRE BL3 3DX
ENGLAND
Telephone: + 44 (0) 1204 366 072
Biography: *K's work is concerned with the positive representations of women: women seen as assertive without being viewed as*

aggressive, women seen as natural without being viewed as uncultured, women seen as feminine without being viewed as passive. Her images have been exhibited in a number of leading galleries and have received major awards as well as being published as a range of very personal greetings cards. K specializes in people, black and white and hand colouring and her work is applicable to editorial, advertising and fashion as well as being bought as fine art.

Portraits: pp 69, 143

Photographer: **MARC JOYE**
Address: BVBA PHOTOGRAPHY JOYE
BURSSELBAAN 262
1790 AFFLIGEM
BELGIUM
Telephone: + 32 (0) 53 66 29 45
Fax: + 32 (0) 53 66 29 52
Biography: *After studying film and TV techniques I turned over to advertising photography, where I found I had a great advantage in being able to organize the shoots. Now, I always prepare my shoots like a movie, with story boards to get the sales story into the picture.*

Portraits: pp 18–19, 123

Photographers: **BEN LAGUNAS AND ALEX KURI**
Address: BLAK PRODUCTIONS PHOTOGRAPHERS
MONTES HIMALAYA 801
VALLE DON CAMILO
TOLUCA
MEXICO CP 50140
Telephone/Fax: + 52 (72) 17 06 57
Biography: *Ben and Alex studied in the USA, and are now based in Mexico. Their photographic company, BLAK Productions, also provides full production services such as casting, scouting, etc. They are master photography instructors for Kodak; their editorial work has appeared in international and national magazines, and they also work in fine art, with exhibitions and work in galleries. Their work can also be seen in the* The Golden Guide, *the* Art Directors' Index, *and other publications. They work all around the world for a client base which includes advertising agencies, record companies, direct clients and magazines.*

Portraits: pp 23, 85

Photographer: **LEWIS LANG**
Address: 83 ROBERTS ROAD
ENGLEWOOD CLIFFS
NEW JERSEY
07632 USA
Telephone: + 1 (0) 201 567 9622
Biography: *I began my career as a film maker, making commercials and documentaries for both broadcast and cable TV. A friend of mine, back in 1983, suggested I use 35mm photography to teach myself about lighting and composition – I ended up loving photography and leaving film making. Since then I've been a free-lance journalist, a fashion photographer, a fine art photographer, working on my own surrealistic of people and still lifes. Some of my fine art photographs are in* Successful Black and White Photography *by Roger Hicks and both my writing and my images have appeared in* Shutterbug, *the third largest photo magazine in the world.*

Portraits: pp 43, 87, 111, 130–131, 140–141

Photographer: **PETER LAQUA**
Address: MARBACHERSTRASSE 29
78048 VILLINGEN
GERMANY
Telephone: + 49 (0) 7721 (0) 305 01
Fax: + 49 (0) 7721 303 55
Biography: *Born in 1960, Peter Laqua studied portraiture and industrial photography for three years. Since 1990 he has had his own studio. A prizewinner in the 1994 Minolta Art Project, he has also had exhibitions on the theme of Pol-Art (fine art photography) and on the theme of 'Zwieback' in Stuttgart in 1992.*

Portraits: pp 88, 146–147

Photographer: **HARRY LOMAX**
Address: ROWDECROFT
ROWDE
DEVIZES,
WILTS SN10 1SN
ENGLAND
Telephone: + 44 (0) 1380 828 907
Fax: + 44 (0) 1380 828 507
Mobile Phone: + 44 (0) 385 302 317
Biography: Industrial and commercial photographer but specializing in architecture and buildings with especial emphasis on food and drinks industry. Main commission is to the designer and/or architect where the mood and style in particular of the interior needs to be brought out. Has produced work for many well-known clients in the brewing industry and related industries, travelling all over the UK and onto the continent.
Portraits: pp 26–27, 45

Photographer: **RUDI MÜHLBAUER**
Address: KREILERSTRASSE 13A
81673 MÜNCHEN
GERMANY
Telephone: + 49 (0) 89 432 969
Biography: *Geboren 1965, fotografiert seit frühester Kindheit, Ausbildung in Fotografenhandwerk, Spezialgebiete: Werbung, Stills, Landschaft, Reportage. Arbeit zur Zeit am Computer (Electronic Imaging und Retouching) für verschiedene Kunden und Werbeagenturen.*
Portraits: pp 21, 139

Photographer: **MAURIZIO POLVERELLI**
Address: 75 47044 IGEA MARINA (RN)
ITALY
Telephone: + 39 (0) 541 33 08 81
Fax: + 39 (0) 541 33 09 81
Biography: *Born in Rimini 30 years ago. He wanted to be a photographer even as a child, and studied photography in Milan at the European Institute of Design followed by working as an assistant to Adriano Brusaferri, who specializes in food. In 1990 he opened his own studio in Rimini. Since then he has had some important advertising clients such as the Mario Formica calendar. Some of the images from this were exhibited in the Modern Art Gallery in Bergamo and in*

London. At present he works mainly in Rimini; in Milan he is represented by Overseas Agency.
Portrait: p 115

Photographer: **DOLORS PORREDON**
Address: C/GIRONA – 9
GRANOLLERS
BARCELONA
SPAIN
Telephone: + 34 (0) 3 870 37 95
Fax: + 34 (0) 3 879 67 97
Biography: *Nacida en Granollers (Barcelona) en 1949. Se inicia en 1972 do forma autodidactica. Hizo reportajes de caracter politico y humanistico en Africa y en paises orientales centrados en el retrato de la figura humana. Actualmente colabora con empresas do imagen, moda, y como ponente en copngresos fotográficos con el retrato de la infancia y la maternidad como temas principales principales. Su trabajo ha sido publicado en diarios, Revistas Fotográficas Españolas y estranjeras, y en programas de TV. Ha espuesto desde 1985 hasta hoy en las principales ciudades Españolas y en Paris, Edimburgo, Colonia y Bruselas. Representó a España en el Congfreso Mundial de Fotografia de la Associación GNPP de Fotogrtafos Franceses en Ajaccio (Corcega) en 1990.*
Portraits: pp 25, 107, 109, 125, 126–127

Photographer: **MASSIMO ROBECCHI**
Address: 44 BOULVECARD D'ITALIE
MC 98000 MONACO
MONTECARLO
Telephone/Fax: + 33 93 50 18 27
Mobile: + 39 (0) 335 37 00 00 (GSM)
Biography: *Thirty-five year old Italian photographer. I moved to Monaco after several years working in Italy. Specialist in people and*

still life, represented world-wide by Pictor International for stock photos.
Portraits: pp 49, 71

Photographer: **TERRY RYAN**
Address: TERRY RYAN PHOTOGRAPHY
193 CHARLES STREET
LEICESTER LE1 1LA
ENGLAND
Telephone: + 44 (0) 116 254 46 61
Fax: + 44 (0) 116 247 0933
Biography: *Terry Ryan is one of those photographers whose work is constantly seen by a discerning pubic without receiving the credit it deserves. Terry's clients include The Boots Company Ltd., British Midlands Airways, Britvic, Grattans, Pedigree Petfoods, the Regent Belt Company, Volkswagen and Weetabix to name but a few. The dominating factors in his work are an imaginative and original approach. His style has no bounds and he can turn his hand equally to indoor and outdoor settings. He is meticulous in composition, differential focus and precise cropping, but equally, he uses space generously where the layout permits a pictorial composition. His work shows the cohesion one would expect from a versatile artist: he is never a jack of all trades, and his pictures are always exciting.*
Portrait: pp 112–113

Photographer: **ALAN SHELDON**
Pager: + 44 (0) 181 840 7000
Code: 0392243
Biography: *I photograph people. For the last few years I have been specializing more and more in celebrity shots, with a lot of emphasis on videos, CD, press and PR: clients include Carlton, ES magazine, Virgin, Absolut Vodka, and Planet Hollywood. I shoot at parties, on location, and in the studio. In my personal work, I've been heavily influenced by Avedon, though when I was an assistant I also worked with big names like Annie Leibowitz, and that I eaves its traces too. In 1996 I am planning to take a portable studio to Morocco to photograph Berber tribes, with a view to an exhibition.*
Portraits: pp 29, 31, 33, 35, 53, 55, 57, 59, 73, 133

mostly in Europe: London, Paris and Geneva. After a year at Toronto's Ryerson University in 1969, he opened his own studio in Toronto in 1970, but in 1989 he gave up his large studio and full time staff, the better to operate on an international level.

He has constantly been in the forefront of beauty and fashion photography, both advertising and editorial, and since 1982 he has also been directing television commercials. He has won numerous awards: Clios for advertising in the US, Studio Magazine awards, National Hasselblad awards, awards in the National Capic Awards Show. His work has appeared in magazines in Japan, the United States, Germany, and Britain as well as Canada.

Portraits: pp 63, 103

Photographer: **FRANK P. WARTENBERG**
Address: LEVERKUSENSTRASSE 25
         HAMBURG
         GERMANY
Telephone: + 49 (0) 40 850 83 31
Fax: + 49 (0) 40 850 39 91
Biography: I began my career in photography alongside my law degree, when I was employed as a freelance photographer to do concert photos. I was one of the first photographers to take pictures of Police, The Cure and Pink Floyd in Hamburg.

After finishing the first exam of my degree, I moved into the area of fashion, working for two years as an assistant photographer. Since 1990 I have run my own studio and am active in international advertising and fashion markets. I specialize in lighting effects in my photography and I also produce black and white portraits and erotic prints.

Portraits: pp 37, 39, 91, 93, 95, 97, 135

Photographer: **STU WILLIAMSON**
Address: CHAPEL COTTAGE
         COVENTRY ROAD
         FLUSHING
         CORNWALL TR11 5TX
         ENGLAND
Telephone/Fax:+ 44 (0) 1326 373 885
Mobile: + 44 (0) 860 210 052
Biography: A former session drummer, Stu turned professional photographer in 1981 and has since won most of the major photographic awards in the UK as well as lecturing world-wide for Ilford, Kodak, KJP (Bowens), Pentax, Contax, Lastolite, BIPP and the MPA. In the late 1980s he became very well known for his "Hollywood" make-over style using the Lastolite Tri-Flector which he invented, working in both monochrome and colour.

He now works almost exclusively in monochrome, both commercially and in fine art photography – his clients value his unique way of seeing – and sells to European calendar companies via his London agents.

Portraits: pp 81, 99

Photographer: **CLIVE STEWART**
Address: DES KLEINEBST PHOTOGRAPH CC
         CNR 10TH ROAD AND 4TH AVENUE
         KEW
         JOHANNESBURG
         SOUTH AFRICA BOX 1921
         BRAMLEY
         JOHANNESBURG 2018
Telephone: 27 (0) 11 882 6005
Fax: 27 (0) 11 882 6072
Biography: At present I work out of a large studio in Johannesburg. Most of the commercial work I do is automotive, with the rest comprised of portraiture and still life. I studied at Natal Technikon for 4 years and received my National Higher Diploma specializing in portraiture. Clients include Toyota, Mazda, Ford, Hyundai, Gilbeys, Allied Bank.

Portrait: p 67

Photographer: **STRUAN**
Address: 60 HERBERT AVENUE
         TORONTO
         ONTARIO M4L 3P9
         CANADA
Telephone: + 1 (0) 416 698 6768
Fax: + 1 (0) 416 698 3338
Biography: "Intuition, simplicity and passion – these are the ingredients I use to create the images that keep me on the edge."
The early part of Struan's life was spent

ACKNOWLEDGMENTS

For this, the third series of PRO-LIGHTING books, we must as ever give our greatest and most heartfelt thanks to all the photographers who gave so generously of pictures, information and time. We hope we have stayed faithful to your intentions, and we hope you like the book, despite the inevitable errors which will have crept in. It would be invidious to single out individuals, but it is an intriguing footnote that the best photographers were often the most relaxed, helpful and indeed enthusiastic about the series – though this is not the same thing as saying they were the ones with the most time to spare.

We also owe a considerable debt to Brian Morris, whose idea the series was, and we should like to thank the manufacturers who supplied the lighting equipment illustrated at the beginning of the book – Photon Beard, Strobex and Linhof and Professional Sales (importers of Hensel flash) – as well as the other manufacturers who support and sponsor many of the photographers in this and other books; we have mentioned them in the text or in the biographies wherever possible. Finally, Colin and Jenny Glanfield of The Plough Studios in London (a major hire studio, call + 44 171 622 1939) were as ever a constant source of help, ideas and introductions.